100% BARCELONA

ⓜ

EL BORNE

100% BARCELONA

There's so much to experience in Barcelona. Where to begin? Of course, you'll want to see Gaudí's architecture and look at art in the MACBA or the Museu Picasso. But also be sure to enjoy authentic tapas, shop on the Passeig de Gràcia, stroll through the old city's little streets, parade on the Ramblas, and see the boats in the harbor. In the evening, take a romantic stroll along the beach, try your luck at the casino, or drink cocktails in a trendy nightclub. This guide will take you by everything you want to see in no time at all: sightseeing, shopping, culinary delights, and adventure. The easy-to-use maps will show you the way.

100% BARCELONA: EXPLORE THE CITY IN NO TIME!

PORT OLÍMPICO

Contents

HOTELS 11

TRANSPORT 18

GRÀCIA 20

L'EIXAMPLE 36

EL GOTICO 56

EL BORNE 76

EL RAVAL 96

BARCELONETA & VILA OLÍMPICA 116

SIGHTS OUTSIDE OF THE CITY CENTER 136

NIGHTLIFE 139

INDEX 142

100% Easy-to-Use

To make this guidebook easy-to-use, we've divided Barcelona up into six neighborhoods and provided a detailed map for each of these areas. You can see where each of the neighborhoods lies in relation to the others on the general map in the front of the book. The letters Ⓐ to Ⓧ will also let you know where to find attractions in the suburbs, hotels, and nightclubs, all described in detail later on in the guidebook.

In the six chapters that follow, you'll find detailed descriptions of what there is to do in the neighborhood, what the area's main attractions are, and where you can enjoy good food and drink, go shopping, take a walk, or just be lazy. All addresses have a number ①, and you'll find these numbers on the map at the end of each neighborhood's chapter. You can see what sort of address the number is and also where you can find the description by looking at its color:

⬤ = sights   ⬤ = shopping

⬤ = food & drink   ⬤ = nice to do

---

6 WALKS

Every chapter also has its own walk, and the maps all have a line showing you the walking route. The walk is described on the page next to the map, and it will take you past all of the most interesting spots and best places to visit in the neighborhood. You won't miss a thing. Not only will you see the most important sights, museums, and parks, but also special little shops, good places to grab lunch, and fantastic restaurants for dinner. If you don't feel like sticking to the route, you'll be able to find your way around easily with the descriptions and detailed maps.

PRICE INDICATION FOR HOTELS AND RESTAURANTS

To give you an idea of hotel and restaurant prices, you'll find an indication next to the address. The hotel prices mentioned are - unless otherwise stated - per double room per night. The restaurant prices are - unless otherwise stated - an indication of the average price of a main course.

THE SPANISH WAY OF LIFE

The Spanish way of life is quite different to what we're used to in the United States and Northern-Europe. Meals are served at different times, and the opening hours of shops vary greatly. Generally, stores are open from ten in the morning to about one-thirty in the afternoon, closing for siesta until five o'clock (except for very touristy spots). At five, they reopen until approximately eight-thirty. During the afternoon, from one to four, is when Spaniards eat, and lunch is the most important meal of the day in Spain. Most restaurants are open both during the afternoon and in the evening, and they often serve very affordable menus at lunchtime. In the evening, restaurants don't open until about eight-thirty. The kitchen usually closes around midnight, and often there's no fixed closing time. If it's busy, the place will remain open until two or three in the morning. Many eateries are closed on Sundays, and making a reservation is almost always necessary.

For the Spanish, eating is a vital part of daily life, and they take extensive time to enjoy their meals. The number of restaurants in town makes it impossible to mention them all, and the quality of the food is generally always good. Tapas are definitely a must when it comes to eating food in Barcelona, and you'll find these delicious morsels all throughout town. Anyone who finds themselves getting hungry by the end of the afternoon grabs a seat at a sidewalk café, orders a cool drink, and picks out some tasty tapas.

August is the main vacation month for the Spanish, and this means that shops and restaurants are often closed. In addition, Barcelona celebrates numerous (national) holidays, and almost all shops are closed on these days. Along with general holidays such as Easter's Maundy Thursday and Good Friday, Easter itself, Whitsun, and Ascension Day, Spain celebrates the following holidays:

1 January	- New Year's Day
6 January	- Epiphany
19 March	- Saint Joseph
23 April	- Saint George (Catalonian holiday)
1 May	- Labor Day
24 June	- Saint John
15 August	- Assumption Festivities of Gràcia
11 September	- La Diada (Catalonian holiday)
12 October	- Columbus Day
1 November	- All Saints' Day
6 December	- Constitution Day
8 December	- Immaculate Conception
25 & 26 December	- Christmas

DO YOU HAVE A TIP FOR US?
We've tried to compile this guide with the utmost care. However, the selection of shops and restaurants can change quite frequently in Barcelona. Should you no longer be able to find a certain address or have other comments or tips for us concerning this guide, please let us know. You'll find our address in the back of the book.

Hotels

In addition to the well-known chains, Barcelona has quite a variety of excellent hotels. As in every city, the rule of thumb here is that you decide yourself just how luxurious and expensive you'd like your accommodations to be. Read on for a number of comfortable suggestions to fit every budget. The hotels are categorized by neighborhood so that you can easily find them on the map in the front of the book. The prices mentioned, unless specified otherwise, are per double room per night, excluding breakfast. Visit *www.barcelona-on-line.com* for a further selection of hotels.

El Borne

(A) The **Park Hotel**, on the edge of Parc Ciutadella, exudes a definite Seventies vibe. From your room, enjoy a view of the beautiful old train station. A pleasant hotel with a pleasant atmosphere.
avenguda marquès de l'argentera, telephone 93 319 60 00, metro barceloneta, price double room per night from €110

(B) **Hotel Banys Orientals** has only been open since 2002, but it's already extremely popular. The location, right in the heart of El Borne, and the 43 stylish rooms make this cozy luxury hotel one of Barcelona's finest.
c. argenteria 37, telephone 93 268 84 60, fax 93 268 84 61, www.hotelbanysorientals.com, metro jaume I, price double room per night from €91

L'Eixample

(C) You'll find **Hotel AC Diplomatic** in the right section of L'Eixample, just next to the Passeig de Gràcia. This modern building belongs to the AC chain, which owns over 50 hotels throughout Spain. There are 211 rooms with modern interiors and countless facilities on hand, including a swimming pool and a gym.
c. pau claris 122, telephone 93 272 38 10, fax 93 272 38 11, www.ac-hotels.com, metro passeig de gràcia, price double room per night from €180

(D) **Claris**, a five-star hotel, is located right in the middle of the Passeig de Gràcia. The inside of this historical building is a fine example of modern architecture. The roof is home to a swimming pool with a view overlooking the city. So, if you can afford this luxury…
c. pau claris 150, telephone 93 487 62 62, fax 93 215 79 70, www.derbyhotels.es, metro passeig de gràcia, price double room per night from €298

El Gotico

(E) The brand-new **H10 Racó del Pi** has 37 rooms, three stars and a great location in the heart of El Gotico, next to the Plaça del Pi and a wonderful little street full of shops.
c. del pi 7, telephone 93 342 61 90, fax 93 342 61 91, www.h10.es, metro universitat, price double room per night from €150

(F) If luxury isn't everything to you, you'll find a nice little guesthouse in **Hostal Mare Nostrum**. You choose to have your own bathroom or to share facilities down the hall. This inn is located right at the heart of the busy Ramblas, so it's not well suited if you're looking for peace and quiet. Breakfast is included in the price.
ramblas 67-sant pau 2, telephone 93 318 53 40, fax 93 318 53 40, metro liceu, price double room per night from €95,

(G) Also on the Ramblas is **Hotel Oriente**. The building, dating back to 1842, has undergone a complete renovation in recent years. Most of the 142 rooms overlook the Ramblas, and if you're in search of a quiet night, be sure to ask for a room at the back of the hotel.
ramblas 45-47, telephone 93 302 25 58, fax 93 412 38 19, www.husa.es, metro liceu , price double room per night from €95

PLAÇA DEL PI

El Raval

(H) Just past the Ramblas, on a charming little square in El Raval, lies **Hotel Sant Agustí**. This is one of Barcelona's oldest hotels, and it's surrounded by the neighborhood's newest restaurants. With 75 rooms and all sorts of extra facilities, this is a quality hotel. Breakfast is also included in the price.
plaça de sant agustí 3, telephone 93 318 16 58, fax 93 317 29 28, www.hotelsa.com, metro liceu, price double room per night from €120

Barceloneta & Vila Olímpica

(I) Without a doubt, Barcelona's most noticeable hotel has to be **Hotel Arts**. The hotel is located in one of the two high towers overlooking the ocean. You can even see it from the airplane. This five-star hotel has all of the luxury you would expect, and it's no small wonder that many celebrities stay here when in town. The penthouse apartments on the top floor run at about €1,200 a night, but luckily the regular rooms are slightly more affordable!
c. marina 19-21, telephone 93 221 10 00, fax 93 221 10 70, www.ritzcarlton.com, metro ciutadella-vila olímpica, price double room per night from €320

(J) You'll really feel like one of the locals if you have your own apartment in Barcelona. **M40** has apartments for rent in the city's small streets. You can make reservations via the Internet, where you can also see photos of the apartments available. A website worth visiting.
c. de la maquinista 40, www.snap.to/barcelona, metro barceloneta, price starting at €465 per week

BASE NAUTICA

BARCELONETA

Transport

Barcelona can easily be reached by bus, train, or taxi from the city's airport. A special bus, the Aerobus shuttle, travels back and forth to Plaça de Catalunya. The bus stop is at the front of the airport building, where you'll also find the taxi stand. The shuttle departs every 15 minutes, and the 30- to 45-minute ride downtown will cost you about €3.50. The train departs from the other end of the airport, and you can travel to Plaça de Catalunya for €2. Trains leave every half an hour, and the ride takes about 25 minutes. If you'd rather take a taxi, you should expect to pay at least €17.50, depending on the time of day and the location of your hotel.

Once you're downtown, you can make use of an extensive **metro** system, which operates under a large portion of the city. This is an easy way to get from A to B, and you can purchase tickets at the entrance to the stations. The best way to travel is to buy a ticket for ten trips, costing €5.60. These tickets can be shared with your fellow travel companions and can be used in all buses. The bus system is, however, somewhat more complicated than the metro, and there's no timetable with extra information available. Every bus stop shows you all of the stops, but always be sure to ask the driver if you're on the right bus. The advantage of traveling by bus is that you see much more of the city than you would in the metro.

Taxis are fairly reasonably priced in Barcelona, and you can easily hail a cab by holding up your hand when one approaches. You can tell whether or not the taxi is occupied by the green light on the roof of the car. The basic fare is €1.10, and for €5 you can travel fairly far. Do keep in mind, however, that prices go up slightly on weekends and after 10pm. You also need to pay an additional surcharge for your luggage.

If you plan on visiting a lot of tourist attractions in one day and you don't feel like walking everywhere, take the **Bus Turistic**. This double-decker, with its open roof, will drive you along red and blue routes, past all major attractions. You can get off and on the bus whenever you want. This is an easy way to get a quick impression of the city and to visit attractions located somewhat out of the way. A daily ticket costs €11, and a two-day ticket will set you back €14.

BICICLOT

Gràcia

Gràcia is like a small village within the bustling city - you can easily observe local living. The neighborhood is sandwiched between Parc Güell and Avenguda Diagonal. One thing you'll notice when walking here is that the area is more or less a connected chain of small city squares. These serve as meeting places for Gràcia's inhabitants. Folks make time for a small chat around a playground, seated on one of many benches, or in one of the many neighborhood bars and cafés. In any event, there always seems to be a relaxed atmosphere. Mostly young people live in this neighborhood, due to

the fact that the rent here is, on average, lower than in other parts of the city. It also makes Gràcia attractive to young entrepreneurs, resulting in a wide array of little shops and restaurants. If you're here in the third week of August, be sure to experience Gràcia's annual neighborhood festivities. Every year, all of Barcelona looks forward to the proceedings!

6 Musts!

Parc Güell

Take a morning stroll
in Parc Güell.

Casa Vicens

Have a look at
Casa Vicens.

Terra

Eat a delicious sandwich
on the terrace at Terra.

Naftalina

Try clothes on
at Naftalina.

Bar Kastola

Drink a vitamin shake
at Bar Kastola.

Café del Sol

Drink a beer at
Café del Sol.

○ **Sights**
○ **Shopping**

● **Food & drink**
○ **Nice to do**

PARC GÜELL ①

③ CASA VICENS

Sights

(1) **Parc Güell** was designed by Gaudí in the period between 1900 and 1914. He moved here himself in 1906, and since 1922, the city has been the park's proprietor. Escape Barcelona's hustle and bustle, and enjoy the most spectacular panorama of the city while up on the hill. Rest your feet, and sit on one of the beautiful mosaic benches in the large square. The series of columns upon which the square rests has a very colorful ceiling with various mosaic depictions of suns and stars.
c. d'olot, open mon-sun 10am-6pm (until 7pm in mar, apr and oct, until 8pm may-sep), metro lesseps

(2) **Museu Gaudí** is located at the beginning of Park Güell. Gaudí actually lived in this house, and some of his belongings are still on display here, such as drawings and furniture. Some rooms have been retained in the original style.
c. del carmel, telephone 93 284 64 46, open mon-sun 10am-6pm (until 7pm in mar, apr and oct, until 8pm may-sep), admission €2.40, metro lesseps

(3) One of Gaudí's first important constructions is **Casa Vicens**. This house was built between 1883 and 1888. Notice the manner in which the colored tiles and stones are combined, both on the exterior and the interior.
c. de les carolines 22, open mon-fri 11am-2pm and 4pm-6pm, sat-sun 11am-2pm, admission €7.50, metro fontana

Food & drink

(6) **Bar Terra** has a wonderful terrace serving equally wonderful sandwiches. Recline in style under a parasol, dining on a warm cream cheese sandwich and all sorts of vegetables. The patrons are of all ages, and it seems like everybody knows each other here.
plaça de la virreina 5, telephone 93 283 66 95, open mon-sun 9am-1.30am, sandwiches €3, metro fontana

(7) **Pas de la Virreina** is another recommended spot for lunch or dinner. Outside, on the terrace, you'll be served in a typically Spanish manner: by a waiter who, while slaloming between busy tables and chairs, still has the time for a little conversation. The menu includes both meat and fish dishes.
c. de torrijos 53, telephone 93 237 37 13, open mon-sat 1pm-4pm and 9pm-midnight, menu price €8, metro fontana

(8) Don't walk by **Cantina Machito** without popping in. Its cheerful colors are inviting. Inside find a small restaurant, as authentically Mexican as can possibly be. Tortillas, guacamole, deliciously spiced meat, and fajitas, all served with a coronita.
c .de torrijos 47, telephone 93 217 34 14, open daily 1pm-6pm and 7pm-2am, price €6, metro fontana

(11) **Bar Kastola's** walls are decorated by the customers who come here. Feel like sharing your thoughts? Grab some chalk, and scribble on the wall! After that, kick back and relax in one of the wicker chairs, sipping on a delectable fruit shake.
c. de la perla 22, telephone 93 771 91 98, open daily noon-1am, price €4, metro fontana

BAR TERRA ⑥

PAS DE LA VIRREINA

⑦ PAS DE LA VIRREINA

⑯ **Café del Sol** is world-famous in Gràcia, It's always busy here, both inside and outside, where you can enjoy a drink or two on the little square. This square also plays a major role during Gràcia's festivities when it's filled with the celebrating masses, which can be heard from miles around.

plaça del sol 16, telephone 93 415 56 63, open daily 1pm-3am, metro gràcia

⑰ At **La Gavina**, everyone sits next to each other on little stools at small wooden tables, their favorite pizza gracing the plate in front of them. Pizza is the only thing you can eat here, but they're made to order: Any topping and anything is possible.

c. de ros de olano 17, telephone 93 415 74 50, open tue-sun 2pm-8pm, price €7, metro fontana

⑲ **Mario** also serves pizzas - a quick snack for those on the move. Just order a Pizza Margarita or one with Roquefort or maybe one with tomato and pesto, and quickly look for a chair or a spot in the sun to gobble it all up.

plaça de rius i taulet 11, telephone 93 416 10 97, open mon-fri 11am-5pm, sat-sun 11am-3am, price €4, metro gràcia

⑳ **Taverna Estrella de Gràcia** is a classic. During the day, come here for a tasty lunch. In the evening, the place turns into a cozy bar, thankfully lacking irritating fluorescent lighting. In short, a fine place to end your day with a little nightcap.

c. de goya 9, telephone 93 217 62 28, open mon-thu 2pm-2am, fri-sat 2pm-1am, menu price €7.50, metro gràcia

Shopping

④ **Modart** is a little shop where they only sell handmade outfits. The two designers behind this fashionable clothing line are Jose Rivera and Carme Trias. Daring trousers with a unique print for him, a provocative evening gown for her, or maybe just nice and casual for both... A versatile duo.
c. d'astúries 34, telephone 93 238 07 86, open mon-sat 11am-2pm and 5pm-9pm, metro fontana

⑤ **do.bella** is a cute little shop where owner Marta Lusilla hand-makes all sorts of jewels. You'll find nice bead necklaces, earrings, and even matching handbags and scarves. Take a good look at the detailed designs.
c. d'astúries 43, telephone 93 237 38 88, open mon 5pm-8.45pm, tue-sat 10.30am-1.45pm and 5pm-8.45pm, metro fontana

⑨ **Pintada** is a clothing store selling hand-painted children's wear. It also offers bags, tablecloths, shoes and many other items. The connecting thread? Original design. You can even take a course here if you want to learn how to decorate clothing yourself.
c. de torrijos 52, telephone 66 045 10 77, open mon 5pm-8.30pm, tue-sat 10.30am-1.30 pm and 5pm-8.30pm, metro fontana

⑩ Take the time to have a close look at each separate article of clothing that **Naftalina** sells and discover that these seemingly basic creations are embellished with subtle and completely original details.
c. de la perla 33, telephone 93 237 25 67, open mon 6pm-9pm, tue-sat 11am-2pm and 6pm-9pm, metro lesseps

⑫ **Jordi Olivé Saperas**'s shop fronts his design studio. He clearly loves cheerful colors, crazy prints and unique materials. Have you ever seen a jacket made out of a fruit-printed plastic tablecloth? Very daring, and certainly one of a kind.
c. de la perla 20, telephone 93 218 20 40, open mon-sat 11am-2pm and 5pm-9pm, metro lesseps

⑬ **Ninas** is owned by an American who has settled in Barcelona.
Her collection is full of subdued colors, and she'll tailor any piece of clothing
on the spot, in case it doesn't fit you perfectly. An artist and friend of the
owner has been allowed to display his hand-made dolls and animals in the
shop. A delight.
*c. de verdi 39, telephone 93 218 60 66, open mon 5pm-9pm, tue-sat 11am-
2pm and 5pm-9pm (thu-sat until 9.30 pm), metro lesseps*

⑭ **Freya** stocks beaded necklaces in all shapes and sizes. There's
enough choice to ensure you walk away with something truly magnificent.
Aside from beads, they also sell other delicate objects made out of tin,
silver, plastic and rubber.
*c. de verdi 17, telephone 93 237 36 98, open mon-sat 11am-2pm and 5pm-
9pm, sun 5pm-9pm, metro fontana*

⑮ **Suite** only sells clothing conceived by Spanish designers, including
Marta r Gustems, the owner of the shop, along with La Casita de Wendy,
Monica Sarabia, and others. Guaranteed originals!
*c. de verdi 3-5, telephone 93 210 02 47, open mon 5pm-8.30pm, tue-sat
10.30am-2pm and 5pm-8.30pm,metro fontana*

⑱ **Món de Mones** is an ideal place to buy presents. Especially for people
who already have everything. The shop, like many others in this neighborhood, is tiny and is packed full with jewelry, clothes and other items
to rummage through. Yes, you will leave with something.
*c. dels xiquets de valls 9, telephone 93 415 60 51, open mon-fri 3pm-9pm,
sat 11am-2pm and 3pm-9pm, metro fontana*

Gràcia

Starting at metro station Vallcarca, follow the signs to Parc Güell ①. Take the stairs to the park. The further up the park's paths you venture, the more beautiful your view of the city will be. Be sure to take a bottle of water with you, as it can be exhausting on a warm day. Leave the park via the entrance, where you'll also find the museum ②. Take a right, and head downhill on c. de Larrard. Take a right onto Travessera de Dalt, and cross at the first traffic lights. Walk through c. de Massens, and take a right onto c. de Sant Salvador. Walk the whole street until you reach c. Gran de Gràcia. The area you're walking in now is predominantly a residential area, connecting the park with the heart of Gràcia. Walk downhill via c. Gran de Gràcia in the direction of one of the many neighborhood bars, and get yourself a cup of coffee. Further down this road, you'll find Gaudí's Casa Vicens ③. Keep going downhill on c. Gran de Gràcia, and take a left onto c. d'Astúries ④ ⑤ Walk until you reach Plaça de la Virreina, and have a delicious lunch ⑥, or cross the road, into c. de Torrijos, where there are other places to grab lunch or do some shopping ⑦ ⑧ ⑨. Now you're in the heart of Gràcia. Take a right into c. de la Perla ⑩ ⑪ ⑫, and head to c. de Verdi, where you'll find some nice shops ⑬ ⑭ ⑮. Keep going downhill, via Plaça Revolució de Setembre de 1868 and c. de Ramón y Cajal, and you'll end up on Plaça del Sol, one of the city's most beautiful squares ⑯ ⑰. This is where you can take a breather, sitting under one of the parasols with the locals. On c. dels Xiquets de Valls, you'll pass a nice jewelry shop ⑱, and finally you'll arrive on the Plaça de Rius i Taulet ⑲. At the end of the square, take a right, and end the afternoon at Taverna Estrella de Gràcia ⑳. There are plenty of other good restaurants here, so make a reservation for the evening.

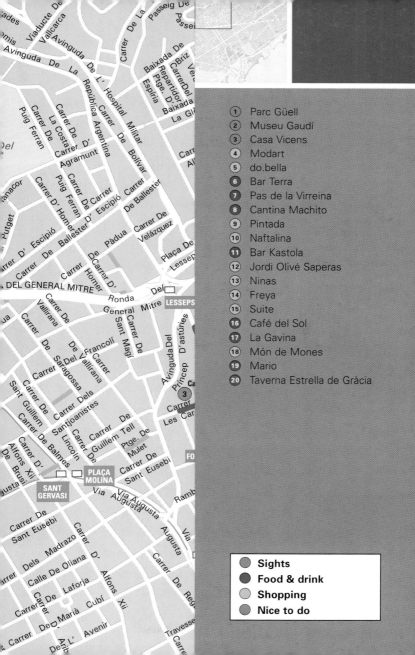

1. Parc Güell
2. Museu Gaudí
3. Casa Vicens
4. Modart
5. do.bella
6. Bar Terra
7. Pas de la Virreina
8. Cantina Machito
9. Pintada
10. Naftalina
11. Bar Kastola
12. Jordi Olivé Saperas
13. Ninas
14. Freya
15. Suite
16. Café del Sol
17. La Gavina
18. Món de Mones
19. Mario
20. Taverna Estrella de Gràcia

- Sights
- Food & drink
- Shopping
- Nice to do

L'Eixample

②

⑦

It's only when walking through L'Eixample that you really notice how simply this area of Barcelona is arranged: long, straight streets, all parallel to each other, intersecting another grid of streets to form right angles. The neighborhood of L'Eixample is comprised of the area between Plaça de Catalunya and Avenguda Diagonal, but is divided into L'Eixample Izquierdo (left) and L'Eixample Derecho (right). In Derecho, you'll find one of Barcelona's most well-known buildings: the Sagrada Familia. L'Eixample doesn't have a central gathering spot, and in fact, the entire neighborhood is located somewhat outside of the heart of Barcelona. If you walk from the Sagrada into down-

town, you'll notice that, above all, L'Eixample is an area of residential houses and access roads. Nevertheless, it's still worth taking the time to casually stroll through the streets. The various styles of houses stand out, with traces of Modernist Antoni Gaudí's influence sprinkled here and there. There are plenty of nice little places to visit in the side streets. Walking from one attraction to the next will require that you cover quite a bit of distance. Rest assured though, there are plenty of spots along the way that are ideal for taking a breather.

6 Musts!

Sagrada Familia

Climb Sagrada Familia's stairs.

Mercat de la Concepció

Shop at Mercat de la Concepció.

Cachitos

Have lunch at Cachitos.

Passeig de Gràcia

Visit Passeig de Gràcia's trendy shops.

La Pedrera

See La Pedrera, and get to know Gaudí better.

Masajes a 1.000

Enjoy a massage for tired legs.

○ **Sights**
○ **Shopping**

● **Food & drink**
○ **Nice to do**

HOSPITAL DE LA SANTA CREU I SANT PAU ①

Sights

(1) The **Hospital de la Santa Creu i Sant Pau**, designed by Domènech and Montaner, consists of 18 different pavilions. Although it actually resembles a park, this is still one of the most important hospitals in Barcelona. It seems that the beautiful surroundings speed up its patients' recovery process.
corner c. de cartegena / c. de sant antoni maria claret, open 24 hours, metro hospital sant pau

(2) You simply have to see the **Sagrada Familia**, one of Antoni Gaudí's most famous and most visited works. Construction began in 1886, and Gaudí (1852-1926) dedicated the last 16 years of his life to the building. The Sagrada is the only cathedral in the world still under construction. If you don't want to climb the innumerable steps to the top, there's always the elevator. The view of Barcelona will delight.
plaça de la sagrada familia, telephone 93 207 30 31, open daily apr-sep 9am-8pm, oct-mar 9am-6pm, admission €6, metro sagrada familia

(5) You'll find the covered market hall of **Mercat de la Concepció** hidden in the middle of a residential area. Stroll leisurely in nice cool surroundings amidst stalls of fish, vegetables, fruit, flowers, and bread in all shapes and sizes. Everything is fresh in this modern looking market, unique in Barcelona.
c. d'aragó 313, telephone 93 457 53 29, open mon-sat 8am-2pm and 4pm-8pm, metro passeig de gràcia

(9) **Passeig de Gràcia** is an attraction in itself. It's as if there's no end to the array of beautiful, luxury shops, the amount of traffic, and the sheer numbers of people spending cash left and right. Nothing has been left to the imagination: benches to rest on, nicely decorated street lamps and wide sidewalks. If you love shopping, you won't want to miss area, where you'll find the crème de la crème of fashion designers, including Chanel, Armani, Max Mara, and Armand Basi.
passeig de gràcia, metro passeig de gràcia

(17) **La Pedrera**, aka **Casa Milà**, was built between 1905 and 1910. Everything you need to know about Gaudí is spread out on five floors. You'll learn a lot about the development of his buildings, and in the 'dream world' on the balcony you'll be able to see his famous 'dolls.' There's also a complete apartment in this museum, decorated in modernist style. It's all equally fascinating!
passeig de gràcia 92, telephone 93 484 59 95, open daily 10am-8pm (summer fri-sat also 9pm-1am), admission €6, metro passeig de gràcia

(21) In 1904, Gaudí built **Casa Batlló**, referred to as the 'house of bones' by Barcelonans. It's a dream-like house, just imagine living there. Unfortunately, it's closed to the public, so you'll have to make do with taking pictures outside.
passeig de gràcia 43, metro passeig de gràcia

(22) You can't miss the **Antoni Tàpies Foundation**. The work of art, constructed from wire, at the top of this modern building is unique. This has been a museum since 1991, showing nearly the complete collection of painter Antoni Tàpies. Next to the museum, there's a library specialized in 20th century art. Here, you'll find regular exhibits of contemporary modern art.
c. d'aragó 255, telephone 93 487 03 15, open tue-sun 10am-8pm, admission €4.20, metro passeig de gràcia

Food & drink

(3) Maybe the interior of this little restaurant seems a bit 'improvised', but don't be dissuaded by that. **Hispanoamericano** is one of those places that Spanish workers frequent for lunch. You'll be able to order a creative daily special for €9 and mingle with the natives.
c. de roger de flor 204, telephone 93 458 48 74, open mon-wed 1pm-5pm, thu-sat 1pm-midnight, menu price €9, metro girona

(4) 'Open the door to your dreams.' That's what it says in pretty curlicue letters on **Cachito**'s window. It seems to be a dollhouse instead of a restaurant: lots of decorations, everything packed in tightly, not many places to sit, and yet very cozy.
c. de roger de flor 204, telephone 62 043 88 89, open mon-sat 9am-9pm, menu price €8, metro girona

(6) Go Dutch in Spain. **Bar Amsterdam**, as the name implies, is a Dutch expatriate's heaven. Spaniards are in the minority, and this bar serves up a number of dishes from Holland, including satay and french fries. Dutch music, (lots of) beer and plenty of talk about Holland's soccer teams in front of the big-screen TV.
c. d'aragó 305, telephone 93 207 37 40, open daily from 6pm, price €8, metro passeig de gràcia

(8) OK, so it's a bit ritzy at **Hostal de Rita**. The tables all look a bit fancy, and well-to-do business people wait until it's their turn and the maître d' shows them to their table. The food, however, is not all that spectacular, but this is a fine enough place for a weekday lunch.
c. d'aragó 279, telephone 93 451 87 07, open daily 1pm-4pm and 8.30pm-midnight, menu price €6.50, metro passeig de gràcia

(11) **Tapa Tapa** is one of many authentic Spanish tapas bars where you can grab some 'picar, picar' all day long. Smoked hams hang from the ceiling, and there's so much to choose from on the menu that it's easier if you just walk in and point to anything that looks good.
passeig de gràcia 44, telephone 93 488 33 69, open daily 7.30 am-midnight, tapas starting at €2, metro passeig de gràcia

CACHITOS ④

⑫ **Il Caffe di Roma** is a great little spot to relax for a while with a delicious cup of Italian coffee. There are many sorts of coffee and tea to choose from, and you'll find Il Caffe di Roma branches throughout Barcelona. They're all equally good for a tasty cappuccino or espresso. *passeig de gràcia 58, telephone 93 487 11 92, open mon-fri 7am-midnight, sat-sun 8am-1am, metro passeig de gràcia*

(20) **Tenorio** is a large restaurant that's always busy, all day long. Breakfast, lunch, dinner: you'll never be sitting alone! The atmosphere is best described as 'swanky', with its fairly modern interior and a 'camarero' leading you to your table. Good food, lots of choice, all for a decent price.
passeig de gràcia 37, telephone 93 272 05 92 or 93 272 05 94, open mon-fri 7.30am-12.30am, sat-sun 9am-1.30am, price €10, metro passeig de gràcia

(24) **Tragaluz** means 'lit dome', and that's precisely the spot underneath which you need to reserve a table: under the lit dome or - in the evening - under the starry skies! Have an aperitif at the bar on the ground floor, and be sure to people watch as fashionable couples enter through the front door.
passatge de la concepció 5, telephone 93 48706 21, open daily 1.30pm-4pm and 8.30pm-midnight, price €15, metro diagonal

(25) The outside of **Madrid-Barcelona** already looks cozy, with all of its shimmering little lights. Fish lovers and admirers of typical Spanish cuisine definitely need to climb the imposing staircase and dine in.
c. d'aragó 282, telephone 93 215 70 26, open daily 1pm-3.45pm and 8.30pm-11.45pm, price €12, metro passeig de gràcia

(26) **Wok & Bol** is not your standard Chinese restaurant, but one dressed in a modern package. Steamed dim sum, tempura with vegetables or duck from the oven? It's all equally delicious here! This means it'll be hard to make choices, but the advantage is that everything is served in little bowls, making it easier to dip your chopsticks into your neighbor's food as well.
c. de la diputació 294, telephone 93 302 76 75, open mon-sat 1.30pm-3.30pm and 9pm-11.30pm, price €10, metro passeig de gràcia

(27) You wouldn't guess it by looking at the outside, but once inside **Thai Gardens**, you're transported to Asia in no time. Friendly service takes you to your table via a labyrinth of cozy corners, flowers, and plants. Once you've tried the delicious curry, order the exotic fruit as dessert. Just the manner in which it's presented is like eating a painting.
c. de la diputació 273, telephone 93 487 98 98, open sun-thu 12.30pm-4pm and 8.30pm-midnight, fri-sat 12.30pm-4pm and 8.30pm-1am, menu price €20, metro passeig de gràcia

Shopping

(10) One of the most famous handbag shops in Barcelona is **Mandarina Duck**. This branch in particular has a very extensive collection. They also sell a small variety of clothing and jewelry. Simple, but very stylish.
passeig de gràcia 44, telephone 93 488 32 26, open mon-sat 10.30am-8.30pm, metro passeig de gràcia

(13) This large bookstore named **Casa del Libro** really sells everything. The travel section alone is enormous. They also have literature in different languages, art books, children's books, cookbooks, and all the way in the back, a small terrace, offering you the chance to sip a 'café con leche' while you choose what to buy. Wonderful chaos.
passeig de gràcia 62, telephone 93 272 34 80, open mon-sat 9am-9pm, metro passeig de gràcia

(14) If you're a woman on a budget, never ever walk into **System Action**! You won't make it out of the door empty-handed. From pants to skirts, dresses and blouses… There's definitely a lot of choice. And the nice thing is that they seem to have everything in all sizes, especially yours!
passeig de gràcia 44, telephone 93 488 07 54, open mon-sat 10am-8.30pm, metro passeig de gràcia

(15) Without a doubt, this is the most beautiful **Replay** shop in Europe. A spectacular entrance, complete with a fountain, little bridges and other unusual details - and this is a clothing store. Make sure you have a fat wallet, as the clothes are somewhat pricey!
passeig de gràcia, open mon-sat 10am-9am, metro passeig de gràcia

SYSTEM ACTION

(16) Barcelona doesn't have too many essential shops for must-have items, but **DOM** offers you the chance to browse through all sorts of hip articles for your living room, kitchen, and office.

passeig de gràcia 76, telephone 93 487 11 81, open mon-sat 10.30am-8.30pm, metro passeig de gràcia

(18) **Bulevard Rosa** is a shopping mall filled with a variety of interesting stores. You'll find clothing, shoes, jewelry, presents, household articles and of course restaurants. One of the favorites is the clothing store Zastwo, right by the entrance. It stocks everything from Dolce & Gabbana shirts to trendy sneakers for men and women.

passeig de gràcia (between c. d'aragó and c. de valència), open mon-sat 10am-8pm, metro passeig de gràcia

(19) Spanish designer **Armand Basi** makes clothing for men and women. He has a stunning collection, but the prices are quite high. The unfussy and pleasant décor really suits the clothing you'll find hanging here, and the perfume line is recommended.

passeig de gràcia 49, telephone 93 215 14, 21, open mon-sat 10am-8pm, metro passeig de gràcia

Nice to do

(7) Although it's not exactly a given that you'll be able to check your email at four in the morning, it's always possible at **Conectate**. You can't miss this large corner building, as it lights up half the street 24 hours a day, seven days a week.

c. d'aragó 283, open 24 hours a day, metro passeig de gràcia

(23) **Masajes a 1,000** is a pure treat after a long day of walking.
Finally, you can put your feet up and enjoy a massage. For merely 1000 pesetas - maybe they missed the introduction of the euro. Enjoy a wonderful neck and back massage, with a pedicure thrown in! Then you'll leave feeling like a new person. Pay in euro's!

c. de mallorca 233, telephone 93 215 85 85, open daily 7am-1am,
price €6 per 15 minutes, metro passeig de gràcia

MASAJES A 1.000 ㉓

L'Eixample

Starting off at metro Hospital Sant Pau, walk uphill in the direction of the hospital ①. After visiting the hospital's many pavillions, you'll spot the Sagrada Familia ② through the green lane. Have breakfast and a cup of coffee on one of the numerous terraces along the way to the cathedral. Go to the park in front of the cathedral, and enjoy the unique view. Leave via Passatge de Maiol in the direction of c. de València. Take a right, and walk past the many carnecerias and pescaderias (butchers and fishmongers), heading towards Avinguda Diagonal. Across the street and on the corner, you'll find Hispanoamericano ③ and Cachitos ④, two great places to grab lunch. Continue your walk via c. de València, to the large market Mercat Concepció ⑤, recognized by the many flowers in front of the door. Once you leave, on the right walk via c. del Bruc towards c. d'Aragó. Around the corner, to the right, is Bar Amsterdam ⑥, and further down, the Internet café ⑦. Hostal de Rita ⑧ is another good lunch option. Head south, into c. de Roger de Llúria, and take a right at hotel AC Diplomatic, towards Passeig de Gràcia ⑨. Shop or rest ⑩ ⑪ ⑫ ⑬ ⑭ ⑮ ⑯ on the way to Casa Milà ⑰. If you cross at Casa Milà, not only will you pass Gaudí's Casa Batlló ㉑, but also many more seductive shops ⑱ ⑲ ⑳ on your way down the hill. Back on c. d'Aragó, turn right towards the Antoni Tàpies Foundation ㉒. Continue your walk by turning right onto c. de Balmes, towards c. de Mallorca. If you're in need of a foot massage, look no further: Masajes a 1,000 ㉓ is here. Afterwards, enjoy a good meal in one of the many cozy restaurants ㉔ ㉕ ㉖ ㉗ in this area.

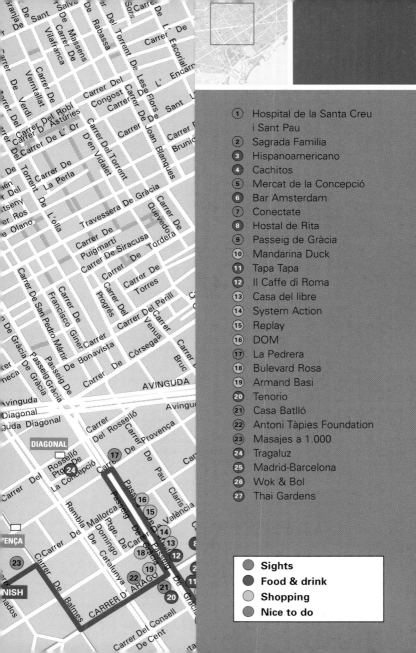

1. Hospital de la Santa Creu i Sant Pau
2. Sagrada Familia
3. Hispanoamericano
4. Cachitos
5. Mercat de la Concepció
6. Bar Amsterdam
7. Conectate
8. Hostal de Rita
9. Passeig de Gràcia
10. Mandarina Duck
11. Tapa Tapa
12. Il Caffe di Roma
13. Casa del libre
14. System Action
15. Replay
16. DOM
17. La Pedrera
18. Bulevard Rosa
19. Armand Basi
20. Tenorio
21. Casa Batlló
22. Antoni Tàpies Foundation
23. Masajes a 1.000
24. Tragaluz
25. Madrid-Barcelona
26. Wok & Bol
27. Thai Gardens

- Sights
- Food & drink
- Shopping
- Nice to do

El Gotico

In Barcelona, El Gotico is the area to the left of the Ramblas, the touristic heart of the city. The Ramblas begins at Plaça de Catalunya and runs all the way down to the harbor. With its many street performers and hodgepodge of stalls selling pets, flowers and otherwise, this is the busiest shopping street in town. In the midst of the excitement, however, keep a watchful eye on your purse as pickpockets are extremely active in this area. It's not difficult to lose your way once you veer off to the right of the Ramblas into a jumble of small streets. Along the way you'll find plenty of quaint shops and bars, especially in the blocks around c. d'Avinyó. There are also more

3

than enough restaurants in this neighborhood. Have a tasty meal and move on to the bar next door for a cold 'cervesa'. You definitely won't be the only tourist in this part of town; this part of Barcelona never seems to sleep!

6 Musts!

Palau de la Música Catalana

Visit the Palau de la Música Catalana.

Santa Església Catedral

See the Gothic cathedral with its idyllic courtyard.

Buenas Migas

Eat lunch at Buenas Migas.

Plaça del Pi & Plaça de Sant Josep Oriol

Stroll through the farmer's market and the art market.

Cafè de l'Acadèmia

Sit on the terrace at Cafè de l'Acadèmia.

C. d'Avinyó

Go shopping around c. d'Avinyó.

○ **Sights**
○ **Shopping**

● **Food & drink**
○ **Nice to do**

PALAU DE LA MÚSICA CATALANA ①

Sights

(1) The **Palau de la Música Catalana** concert hall was constructed by architects Domènech and Montaner, between 1905 and 1908. The colorful building is filled with beautiful mosaics and stained glass windows. To see inside, you'll have to buy a ticket for the tour, which takes place every half hour. Even better is attending one of the concerts held here.
c. de sant francesc de paula 2, telephone 93 295 72 00, open daily 10am-3.30pm (until 6pm in aug), tickets for sale at c. de st. pere més alt 1 9.45pm-3pm, tours 50 minutes, admission €5, metro urquinaona

(3) The **Santa Església Catedral**: you can't and shouldn't miss it. This gigantic building's first stone was laid in 1298, and the last one was set sometime in the 19th century. Once you're inside, it becomes clear how big a role the church still plays in the daily lives of the Spanish. In the chapels, there are many icons of saints with candles burning next to them. This Gothic cathedral's courtyard is also unique, with its geese, orange trees and souvenir shops.
pla de la seu 3, telephone 93 315 15 54, open daily 8am-1.30pm and 4pm-7.30pm, metro jaume I

(5) **Museu Frederic Marès** (1893-1991) is named after a travel-mad sculptor who collected absolutely everything during his journeys. All of these objects, including many paintings, a collection of pipes, cameras, maps and toy soldiers, are now on display here. The museum also has a beautiful terrace in the courtyard during the summer.
plaça de sant lu 5-6, telephone 93 310 58 00, open tue-sat 10am-5pm, sun and holidays 10am-3pm, café d' estiu open apr-sep 10am-10pm, admission €3, www.museummares.bcn.es, metro jaume I

(7) You'll see archeological findings from the last 2,000 years at the **Museu d'Història de la Ciutat**. The museum even houses some of old Barcelona's subterranean remains - definitely worth taking the time to check these out.
plaça del rei s/n, telephone 93 315 11 11, open tue-sat oct-may 10am-2pm and 4pm-8pm, jun-sep 10am-8pm, sun 10am-2pm, admission €3.60, www.museuhistoria.bcn.es, metro jaume I

(23) **Plaça del Pi** and **Plaça de Sant Josep Oriol** are connected to each other, and together they form downtown's coziest square. The square is filled with sidewalk cafés, a gigantic church acting as the centerpiece. On Saturdays there's a farmers' market on the Plaça del Pi, offering all kinds of delicious products. The other square plays host to an art market, where you'll find artists peddling their craft at the beginning of each month.

plaça del pi and plaça de sant josep oriol, metro liceu

Food & drink

(2) If you're hankering for a tasty breakfast or a delicious cup of coffee, look no further than **Tutto Caffe**. You can choose from a multitude of coffee and tea blends, and they also sell them to go. Take some back on the plane and remember good 'ole Barcelona while settling back at home.
via laietana 41, telephone 93 302 08 43, open daily 7am-midnight, price coffee starting at €1, metro urquinaona

(4) Sitting at the sidewalk café at **Bilbao-Berria** will lend you a spectacular view of the cathedral. Also, you'll be able to eat some mouth-watering tapas. Choose your favorites inside, and then take them outside with you for al fresco dining. Street performers contribute to the lively atmosphere.
plaça nova 3, telephone 93 317 01 24, open mon-fri 8am-midnight, sat-sun 8.30am-1am, price tapas €1.50, metro jaume I

(6) **Buenas Migas** serves scrumptious focaccias, pizzas and pies. This is a great address for staving off your growing hunger. Sit on the pleasant terrace, enjoy a piece of delicious chocolate cake, and watch the folks walk by.
bajada santa clara 2, telephone 93 318 13 80, open sun-wed 10am-10pm, thu-sat 10am-midnight, price €5, metro jaume I, another branch is at plaça del bonsuccés 6, telephone 93 412 16 86 or 93 318 37 08, metro catalunya

(10) **Café de l'Acadèmia** is somewhat hidden in a small and idyllic square. This is the place to quietly enjoy an appetizing lunch. How about chicken bathed in a beer sauce? It might sound strange, but it's truly divine!
c. de lledó 1, telephone 93 319 82 53, open mon-fri 1.30pm-4pm and 9pm-midnight, menu price €9, metro jaume I

(11) **Cometacinc** is really hidden. It's located in a beautiful building, has an appealing décor, and the food is quite good. Recipes gathered from different countries are on the menu, as well as are original desserts. Here, close attention is paid to the details. How about the lamb steak with red peppers, eggplant and potato, please?

c. cometa 5, telephone 93 310 15 58, open mon, wed-sun 8pm-1am, price €10, metro jaume I

(17) A favorite place for lunch is **Venus**. This spot provides much-needed quiet away from the maddening crowds. And the prices on the menu are decent. The walls are decorated with colorful art (and the art's for sale). The service is always cheerful, as is the music.

c. avinyó 25, telephone 93 301 15 85, open mon-sat 12am-midnight, menu price €7.50, metro liceu

(18) **Plà** guarantees a wonderful evening. The combinations served may seem a little strange at first: carpaccio of manchego cheese is, after all, not an everyday dish. The menu offers meat or poultry and delicious Japanese food as well. The waiter will patiently help you make your choice from the selection of well-chosen wines and plates.

c. bellafila 5, telephone 93 412 65 52, open sun-thu 9pm-midnight, fri-sat 9pm-1am, price €10, metro jaume I

(19) **Limbo** opened fairly recently, and it's certainly worth a visit. It's hidden away in a small street, and the inside resembles a basement of sorts. Limbo is an exciting mix of old and new, full of intimate corners. The food is good, offering a large variety: meat, fish, and vegetarian.

c. mercè 13, telephone 93 310 76 99, open tue-thu, sun 9pm-midnight, fri-sat 9pm-1am, price €11, metro jaume I

(20) **Los Caracoles** is a Barcelonan institution - a typical Spanish restaurant. The waiter will bring you to your table via the bar and through the kitchen. From outside, you can even see the chickens rotating on a spit. This bird, in fact, plays a central role on the menu. Of typical Catalonian dishes, there are plenty of choices.
c.escudellers 14, telephone 93 302 31 85, open daily 1pm-4.30pm and 8.30pm-11.30pm, price €10, metro liceu

(26) **The Travelbar** is cozy, and here you'll meet people from all four corners of the world. Enjoy the language buzz, seemingly comprised of 20 different foreign tongues, outside on the terrace. You can check your email inside and also register for a weekly pub crawl or city tour.
c. boqueria 27, telephone 93 342 52 52, open mon-fri 9.00 am-2.00 am, sat-sun 9am-3am, www.barcelonatravelbar.com, metro liceu

(28) **Café Shilling** is a true 'grand café', and there aren't too many of those in Barcelona. Great to go to after an afternoon of shopping or for a drink in the evening. Don't be surprised if the male/female quotient is somewhat out of balance, as Schilling is also popular with the gay crowd.
c. ferran 23, telephone 93 317 67 87, open daily 10am-2.30am, metro liceu

Formatge de
cabra amb
romani.
€:20 /kg

Shopping

(8) You'll find pens, diaries, photo albums and notebooks (many are leather-bound) of all shapes and sizes at **Papirum**. The selection is far too vast, but they're all practical items. After all, since everyone needs a personal diary, you might as well buy one that 'wows' them.
baixada de la llibreteria 2, telephone 93 310 52 42, open mon-fri 10am-8.30pm, sat 10am-2pm and 5pm-8.30pm, metro jaume I

(9) **Formatgeria la seu** is a small shop offering different wines, olive oil and various cheeses. Everything is manufactured organically. Free samples are a given.
c. dagueria 16, telephone 93 412 65 48, open mon-sat 10am-2pm and 5pm-8pm, metro jaume I

(12) If you're looking for an original item of clothing, take a peek at **Zsu Zsa**. This small shop is full of exclusive designer clothing. Especially noteworthy are the unique cuts, bizarre fabrics and distinctive finishing touches. They also sell striking accessories, jewelry and purses.
c. avinyó 50, telephone 93 412 49 65, open mon 5pm-9pm, tue-sat 11am-2pm and 5pm-9pm, metro liceu

(13) From clothing to hats, jewelry and handbags: you'll find it all at **Zebra**. The shop assistants are very helpful, and if your size isn't hanging on the rack, there's a good chance they'll be able to find it for you in the design studio in the back. Everything is reasonably priced, considering they're all made in limited quantities.
c. avinyó 46, telephone 93 318 44 58, open mon 5pm-9pm, tue-sat 11am-2pm and 5pm-9pm, metro liceu

⑭ **Loft Avignon** is a great shop with a diverse collection of clothing by well-known designers such as Jean-Paul Gaultier and Helmut Lang. They sell Indian Rose jeans here, so definitely try those on! Male or female - you'll always find a treasure here.
c. avinyó 46, telephone 93 301 24 20, open mon-sat 10.30am-2.30pm and 4.30pm-8.30pm, metro liceu

⑮ **Sita Murt** recently opened the doors to her clothing store, where she sells various designer labels including Esteve, Sita Murt, Save the Queen, and Whistless. You'll find nicebasic items here, but also eyecatching designs. Don't forget to also take a look downstairs.
c. avinyó 18, telephone 93 301 00 06, open mon-fri 10.30am-2pm and 4.30pm-8.30pm, sat 10.30am-8.30pm, metro jaume I

⑯ Just how many pairs of espadrilles do they have in the closet at **La Manual Alpargater**? Too many to count. Suffice it to say - a lot, all in various styles and colors. On the workbench in the back, espadrilles are still sewn by hand. It's nice to see that this old trade is still being practiced today.
c. avinyó 7, telephone 93 301 01 72, open mon-sat 9.30am-1.30pm and 4.30pm-8pm, metro liceu

㉑ **Casa Miranda Martì** is another old little shop, this time packed with wooden and wicker knick-knacks. They sell everything, it seems, but some of it may be a little too bulky to take onto the plane with you. Make room in your carry-on for a sturdy wicker shopping basket.
c. banys nous 15, telephone 93 301 83 29, open mon-sat 9.30am-2pm and 4.30pm-8pm, metro liceu

㉒ **Caelumis** is a bit holy. All of the delicious items you'll end up buying here are made by nuns. You won't be able to pass up the homemade jam, chocolate or wine - if only for the packaging. They even have a small café in the basement where you can 'test' the wares.
c. de la palla 8, telephone 93 302 69 93, open mon-sat 10.30am-2pm and 5pm-8pm, metro liceu

㉔ The **Miró Jeans** shop does indeed belong to Spanish designer Antonio Miró. The austere shop is full of basic and simple clothing, and the Spanish are crazy about every bit of it. Every wardrobe in Spain includes at least one piece by a native designer. And Miró is the choice of many.
c. del pi 11, telephone 93 342 58 75, open mon-sat 10am-9pm, metro liceu

㉕ **Casas** is one of the finest shoe shops in Barcelona - from trendy sneakers to ultra feminine pumps by known brands such as Muxart and the house label Casas. A must for shoe lovers, especially when the sales are on.
c. portaferrissa 25, telephone 93 302 11 32, open mon-sat 10am-9pm, metro pl. catalunya

㉗ **Rey Pez** sells a mixture of beautiful Indian clothing, unique jewelry and attractive artwork. The store is a bit cluttered, but you'll feel supremely lucky when you make a real discovery in some hidden corner.
c. rauric 3, telephone 93 412 30 97, open mon-sat 10.30am-2pm and 4.30pm-8.30pm, sat 10.30am-9pm, metro liceu

El Gotico

At metro Urquinaona take the exit to Via Laietana and enter the c. de Ramon, heading in the direction of the Palau de la Música Catalana ①. You can have a delicious cup of coffee or eat breakfast at Tutto Caffè ② on the Via Laietana. Walking via c. del Doctor Joaquim Pou, you'll arrive at the cathedral ③. To the right of the church is restaurant and tapas bar Bilbao-Berria ④. If you pass the cathedral on the right-hand side, you'll end up on a courtyard filled with artists and musicians. Carry on by taking a left onto c. de la Pietat, and you'll end up on c. dels Comtes, where you'll find the Museu Frederic Marès ⑤. Maybe grab lunch at Buenas Migas ⑥, and afterwards walk down the Baixada de Santa Clara, to the city's historical museum ⑦. Walk right, past Papirum ⑧, into c. de la Dagueria ⑨, and continue until you reach Plaça de Sant Just, where you can rest at one of the sidewalk cafés ⑩. Walk into c. de Lledó, and take a right at c. del Cometa, where you'll find Cometacinc ⑪ on the corner. At the end of the street, you'll find Plaça del Regomir. Continue your walk through c. de Calella, until you reach c. d'Avinyó for some serious shopping ⑫ ⑬ ⑭ ⑮ ⑯. There are also quite a few restaurants all worth your while for dinner in this area ⑰ ⑱ ⑲ ⑳. At the end of c. d'Avinyó, cross the street and take a left onto c. de l'Ave Maria ㉑ ㉒. At the end of the street, you'll end up on two connected squares, the Plaça del Pi and Plaça de Sant Josep Oriol ㉓ ㉔ ㉕ ㉖. Via c. d'Alsina, continue your route downhill onto c. d'en Rauric ㉗, finally ending up on c. de Ferran. Have a drink at Café Shilling ㉘, and make plans for the evening.

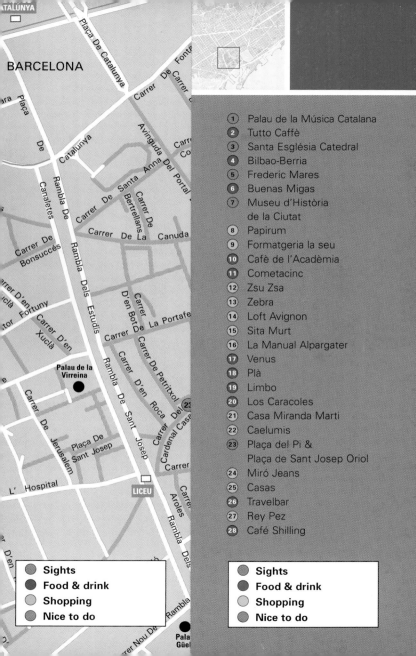

BARCELONA

1. Palau de la Música Catalana
2. Tutto Caffè
3. Santa Església Catedral
4. Bilbao-Berria
5. Frederic Mares
6. Buenas Migas
7. Museu d'Història de la Ciutat
8. Papirum
9. Formatgeria la seu
10. Cafè de l'Acadèmia
11. Cometacinc
12. Zsu Zsa
13. Zebra
14. Loft Avignon
15. Sita Murt
16. La Manual Alpargater
17. Venus
18. Plà
19. Limbo
20. Los Caracoles
21. Casa Miranda Marti
22. Caelumis
23. Plaça del Pi & Plaça de Sant Josep Oriol
24. Miró Jeans
25. Casas
26. Travelbar
27. Rey Pez
28. Café Shilling

Sights
Food & drink
Shopping
Nice to do

Sights
Food & drink
Shopping
Nice to do

El Raval

El Raval is an up-and-coming neighborhood. This area, starting at the Plaça de Catalunya to the right of the Ramblas and stretching all the way to the ocean, wasn't the most vibrant place to venture into in the Seventies and Eighties. The inhabitants were fairly lowclass, and El Raval was rife with prostitution and drug trafficking. Luckily these problems have subsided in recent years, and today's population is much more diverse. The city council has done its best to revitalize the area, making it more attractive for inhabitants and business people. The transformation has really worked well. With its new

4

museums, scores of new little shops and restaurants, El Raval is slowly
turning into a completely new and trendy neighborhood. Some buildings
have been totally renovated while others remain untouched. Remarkably, it's
this combination of the two that really makes for interesting urban planning.

6 Musts!

CCCB & MACBA

Visit the CCCB
and the MACBA.

Gran Teatre del Liceu

Watch a show at
Gran Teatre del Liceu.

Palau Güell

See the Palau Güell.

Els Tres Tombs

Have tapas and beers
at Els Tres Tombs.

Sushi & News

Enjoy sushi at
Sushi & News.

Salsitas

End the day swinging
at Salsitas.

○ **Sights**
○ **Shopping**

● **Food & drink**
○ **Nice to do**

Sights

(1) The **Centre de Cultura Contemporània de Barcelona** (CCCB) was opened in 1994. This is a cultural center offering an assortment of temporary exhibitions, from photography openings to concerts and lectures all related to the city of Barcelona.
c. montalegre 5, telephone 93 306 41 00, open tue, thu-fri 11am-2pm and 4pm-9pm, wed, sat 11am-8pm, sun and holidays 11am-7pm, admission €4, www.cccb.org, metro catalunya

(2) The **Museu d'Art Contemporàni de Barcelona** (MACBA) was opened one year after the CCCB, in 1995. This modern white building, with its many windows in the front, was designed by renowned architect Richard Meier. This museum regularly hosts exhibits by a variety of predominantly Catalan artists.
plaça dels àngels 1, telephone 93 412 08 10, open mon-fri 11am-8pm, sat 10am-8pm, sun and holidays 10am-3pm, admission €6, www.macba.es, metro catalunya

(10) The architecture of the **Palau de la Virreina**, built between 1772 and 1778, has many baroque influences. The palace belongs to the 'generalitat' (the city), and temporary exhibits of modern art are on show. In addition, the building serves as the information center for the city's various museums, performances and courses.
la rambla de sant josep 99, telephone 93 301 77 75, open tue-sat 11am-8pm, sun and holidays 11am-3pm, admission palace tour €3 (wed €1.50), metro catalunya

(11) Each neighborhood has its own covered market, but the **Mercat de la Boqueria** is quite possibly the most unique. This market hall is bubbling with energy all day long. Rich or poor, tourist or authentic Spanish señora, everyone leaves carrying grocery baskets filled with vegetables, fruits, meats, fish and much more.
la rambla 99, open mon-sat 7am-8.30pm, metro liceu

TEATRE DEL LICEU

23 GRAN TEATRE DEL LICEU

㉓ The **Gran Teatre del Liceu** is Barcelona's most famous opera house. In 1994, the building, except for the front façade, was completely destroyed by fire. It wasn't until 1999 that the opera reopened, and with 3,500 seats, it's one of the world's largest theaters. Unfortunately, in spite of all the seats, it's still consistently difficult to get tickets. So, if there are still seats for a performance that appeals to you, don't hesitate: you're sure to have an unforgettable experience!

la rambla 51-59, telephone 93 485 99 00, open for information mon-fri 10am-1pm and 2.30pm-6.30pm, www.liceubarcelona.com, metro liceu

㉔ The **Palau Güell** was built between 1886 and 1890. Eusebi Güell was a good friend of Gaudí's and a big admirer of his work, so it's no wonder that the task of constructing the palace went to Gaudí himself. The building was completely restored to its authentic style in the 90s, and since 1997, visitors have been able to take a guided tour.

c. nou de la rambla 3-5, telephone 93 317 39 74, open mon-sat 10am-8pm, sun and holidays 10am-2pm, admission tour €3, metro drassanes

㉖ **Centre d'Art Santa Mònica** is a center for temporary exhibits of national and international art. From the outside, the building looks impressive with its large glass wall and a pedestrian bridge leading you to the entrance. Inside, downstairs, you'll be able to find tons of information about festivals and the city's museums, as well as the free monthly magazine Metropolitan, which is full of tips and cultural schedules.

ramblas de santa mònica 7, open mon-sat 11am-2pm and 5pm-8pm, sun and holidays 11am-3pm, metro drassanes

㉗ The **Museu de la Cera de Barcelona** is hidden away at the end of the Ramblas. This is a wax museum featuring over 350 personalities. Of course they include Antoni Gaudí, Franco and other Spanish notables.

passeig banca 7, telephone 93 317 26 49, open oct-jun mon-fri 10am-1.30pm and 4pm-7.30pm, sat-sun 11am-2pm and 4.30pm-8.30pm, jul-sep daily 10am-10pm, admission €7, metro drassanes

⑨ **KASPARO**

Food & drink

③ **Pla dels Àngels** is located right next to the MACBA and is a perfect spot for sitting outside at a sidewalk café. This is a great place for lunch, especially when the sun is shining. Don't get me wrong, there's plenty to see inside as well.
c. ferlandina 23, telephone 93 329 40 27, open mon 9pm-11.30pm, tue-sat 1.30pm-4pm and 9pm-11.30pm, menu price €8, metro catalunya

④ **Fragile** is the middle restaurant on this cozy little square. You'll find few tourists here, since many don't expect to find such a good place to eat in this area. The Spanish, however, know how to find Fragile all too well, and this means that you'll be enjoying your meal, sitting among the locals.
c. de la ferlandina 27, telephone 93 442 18 47, open daily 9.30am-2pm, price menu €8, metro catalunya

⑤ **Original** is all the way to the right of the same small square. As at many restaurants in Barcelona, you can choose a lunch menu during the daytime, while ordering à la carte in the evening. For example a delicious soup as a starter, followed by yummy plate of pasta. And you haven't even seen the desserts yet…
c. ferlandina 29, telephone 93 443 29 88, open mon-sat 9am-3am, price menu €8, metro catalunya

⑨ **Kasparo** serves the most delicious sandwiches. The place is a bit hidden in a corner, but this affords you a nice view of the children in the playground.
plaça vicenç martorell 4, telephone 93 302 20 72, open daily 9am-midnight, price menu €9, metro catalunya

⑬ **Ra**'s location, behind the market hall, might not seem ideal, but this is a cozy little place, and the food is both tasty and affordable. And if you enjoy the sport of people watching, you'll be able to pass the seconds since the food is served rather slowly from time to time.
psg 1800 (plaça de la garduña), telephone 93 301 41 63, open mon-sat 9am-1.30pm, price menu €8, metro liceu

⑭ **Iposa** is an intimate restaurant with friendly service and menus for a mere €5. That's even a fantastic price by Barcelona standards. However, price isn't the only unique thing about Iposa: Every Friday and Saturday, from 4pm to 10pm, the restaurant has an on-site masseur. He'll gladly give you the perfect treatment between courses.

c. floristes de la rambla 14, telephone 93 318 60 86, open mon-sat 1pm-3am, price menu €5, www.bariposa.com, metro liceu

⑯ **Muebles Navarro** is the sort of café where you can spend hours by yourself enjoying only the company of a good book. The interior hints at the building's former life as a furniture store. All kinds of benches, chairs and tables are jumbled up in the café, adding to the place's unique charm.

c. de la riera alta 4-6, telephone 93 457 40 99, open tue-thu 5pm-midnight, fri-sun 5pm-2.30am, metro liceu

⑰ **Sesamo** is one of the welcomed new places to visit in El Raval. This is a restaurant serving vegetarian food, and I must say, the most delicious culinary creations come out of the kitchen. Don't skip dessert here. The chocolate cake is one of the best around. After dinner, continue relaxing at the bar in the front.

c. sant antoni abat 52, telephone 93 441 64 11, open mon noon-6pm, wed-thu, sun 12am-1am, fri-sat 12am-2.30am, price menu €7, metro sant antoni

⑱ **Els Tres Tombs** is well known in Barcelona, occupying an entire street corner. The sun shines here all day, and you can enjoy tasty tapas at lunch in the company of the 'in-crowd'. Don't look surprised if someone strikes up a conversation with you.

ronda de sant antoni 2, telephone 93 443 41 11, open daily 6am-3.30am, metro sant antoni

8€ menú

primeros
- Ensalada RA
- Gazpacho
- Pasta fria con gambas

segundos
- Pollo con guacamole
- Bacalao con salsa verde
- Verduras

sugerencia
CUIDADO

(22) **Rita Blue** is a cheerful restaurant, perfect for lunch or dinner, a drink at the bar or dancing on a Sunday evening. In any event, it's extremely popular with young and trendy Barcelonans, and the place is always busy. The menu is huge, and the cooks turn every dish into a delicious work of art.
plaça sant agusti 3, telephone 93 342 40 86, open daily 1pm-3am, price menu €8, metro liceu

(25) You enter hip **Salsitas** via a long, narrow lounge. You arrive in the restaurant all the way in the back, and you make your choice from an extensive selection of dishes. The food is fine, but you won't get the chance to remain seated for a long period of time. At midnight, the place turns into a nightclub, and people dance until the early morning hours.
c. nou de la rambla 22, telephone 93 318 08 40, open mon-sat 12am-4pm and 8pm-midnight, price €9, metro liceu

(28) **Sushi & News** is a favorite among admirers of Japanese cuisine. The delicious, fresh sushi is prepared right in front of you, and there are plenty of soups, salads, noodles and other Japanese specialties on the menu. Don't be alarmed by the folks hanging around on the street. C. de santa mònica is often frequented by prostitutes and their johns.
c. santa mònica 2 bis, telephone 93 318 58 57, open tue-sat 1.30pm-4.30pm and 8.30pm-12.30am, price €7, metro drassanes

Shopping

(6) You need an hour to get a good look at everything at **Forvm Ferlandina**. This jewelry mall presents pieces by artists from all over Europe. Some of the items are magnificent, and therefore, the prices aren't low. Should you happen to have your own design for a jewelry item, they'll be glad to make the object for you in the studio located in the back.
c. ferlandina 31, telephone 93 441 80 18, open tue-fri 10.30am-2pm and 5pm-8.30pm, sat 11am-2pm, www.forvmjoies.com, metro universitat

(7) **Gimenez & Zuazo** is daring. You'll be the absolute star of the evening if you wear a creation designed by owners Marta and George. But let's be honest: You don't wear styles like these unless you've got a lot of courage. Do, however, take a look, even if it's only to be inspired.
c. elisabets 20, telephone 93 412 33 81, open mon-sat 10.30am-2.30pm and 5pm-8.30pm, metro catalunya

(8) **B.Huno** sells simple, stylish designs fashioned from lovely materials. Aside from clothing, the shop has a small amount of jewelry, purses and shoes. It's almost unimaginable that you won't find just a little something to take back home with you from here.
c. elisabets 18, telephone 93 412 63 05, open mon-sat 10.30am-2.30pm and 4.30pm-8.30pm, metro catalunya

(12) **Escribà** is located in a corner building, and you can clearly see Gaudí's influence in the architecture. This pàtisserie has been around since 1906, and almost anyone who knows there way around Barcelona knows how to find Escribà. Almost no one can resist buying something sweet here, surprising since the Spanish don't eat that many pastries. If you can't wait to sample before you reach your hotel, you can also eat your goodies in the back, accompanied by a piping hot cup of coffee.
la rambla de les flors 83, telephone 93 301 60 27, open daily 8.30am-9pm, metro liceu

(19) **Lailo** sells all sorts of vintage clothing, handbags, shoes and other accessories. Take a good look, and you'll find some really spectacular vintage dresses with just enough flare to make a lasting impression at the next party.
c. riera baixa 20, telephone 93 441 37 49, open mon-sat 10.30am-2pm and 4.30pm-8.30pm, metro liceu

(20) **Discos Edison's** is a small store completely filled with old records, cassettes and CDs. Don't come in here looking for the latest hits; 'oldies' are what they specialize in. So, if you're looking for that long-lost Clash album, chances are pretty good that you'll find it here!
c. riera baixa 9, telephone 93 329 23 15, open mon-sat 10.30am-2pm and 4.30pm-8.30pm, metro liceu

(21) **Mies & Felj** offers a fine collection of new and vintage clothing. Their summer floral-printed dresses are always very popular.
c. riera baixa 4-5, telephone 93 442 07 55, open mon-sat 11am-2pm and 5pm-8.30pm, metro liceu

Nice to do

(15) The **Antic Hospital Santa Creu** was Barcelona's largest and most well known hospital in the 15th century. Today, the buildings house the Catalunya library, the Institute for Catalan Studies and a chapel presenting temporary exhibitions. Everyone is welcome to take a stroll through the beautiful gardens, and this is a nice spot to in relax for a while. Stroll and chill.
c. de l'hospital 56, chapel open tue-sat 12am-2pm and 4pm-8pm,
sun 12am-3pm, metro liceu

El Raval

Starting at metro station Plaça de Catalunya, take c. dels Tallers, known for its many music shops. Having arrived at c. de Valldonzella, you'll be able to see the Centre de Cultura Contemporània de Barcelona ① and the MACBA ②. These two guarantee a morning's worth of discovering art. To the left, in front of the MACBA, you'll find a number of culinary addresses that will help you start the day ③ ④ ⑤ ⑥. Later on, continue your walk to c. d'Elisabets, passing Gimenez & Zuazo ⑦ and B.Huno ⑧. Down the road, on the Plaça de Vincenç Martorell, you'll find a nice sidewalk café at Kasparo ⑨. If you walk through c. del Bonsuccés, you'll find yourself back on the Ramblas. Further downhill, you'll pass the Palau de la Virreina ⑩, the Mercat de la Boqueria ⑪ and Barcelona's most famous patisserie ⑫ on your right-hand side. Two quaint restaurants are hidden at the back of the covered market halls ⑬ ⑭. Walking down c. les Floristes de la Rambla, you'll end up on c. del Carme. Turn left onto this street, one of the main roads of El Raval. Casually stroll past all of the little neighborhood shops. You'll be able to rest your feet at the Antic Hospital Santa Creu ⑮, sitting on a bench in the garden. There are a number of places for dinner near the hospital ⑯ ⑰ ⑱, and you'll find excellent vintage clothing stores in c. de la Riera Baixa ⑲ ⑳ ㉑. Head back in the direction of the Ramblas via c. de l'Hospital ㉒, and take a right to get to the Gran Teatre del Liceu ㉓. Continue, heading towards the ocean until you reach c. Nou de la Rambla. You'll see the Palau Güell ㉔ to your left. Turn back, passing Salsitas ㉕, in the direction of the Ramblas. The last little stretch of the Ramblas is home to the Centre d'Art Santa Mònica ㉖ and the wax museum ㉗. If you, however, have already seen enough, go grab some of the city's most delicious sushi ㉘.

1. Centre de Cultura Contemporània de Barcelona CCCB
2. Museu d'Art Contemporàni de Barcelona MACBA
3. Pla dels Àngels
4. Fragile
5. Original
6. Forvm Ferlandina
7. Gimenez & Zuazo
8. B.Huno
9. Kasparo
10. Palau de la Virreina
11. Mercat de la Boqueria
12. Escribà
13. Ra
14. Iposa
15. Antic Hospital Santa Creu
16. Muebles Navarro
17. Sesamo
18. Els Tres Tombs
19. Lailo
20. Discos Edison's
21. Mies & Felj
22. Rita Bleu
23. Gran Teatre del Liceu
24. Palau Güell
25. Salsitas
26. Centre d'Art Santa Mònica
27. Museu de Cera de Barcelona
28. Sushi & News

- ● Sights
- ● Food & drink
- ● Shopping
- ● Nice to do

El Borne

El Borne is one of the most popular areas of Barcelona at the moment.
This is where it's all going on! El Borne has the best restaurants, the
newest shops, and plenty to offer culture-wise, and it's all happening in
the neighborhood between Parc de la Ciutadella and Via Leitana. Seemingly
everybody wants to live here, especially young people and aspiring artists.
That's why you can find small shops and studios with original clothing,
jewelry, or art nestled between small, authentic stores selling colorful pottery.
Popular, but still a lot quieter than in the city center, where it seems to be
Saturday afternoon every day of the week. You'll find many little restaurants

5

in the countless small streets, ranging from fusion to Spanish, Italian, and Basque cuisine. Some are so small that they resemble a living room more than a restaurant. Be sure to make reservations, as everything fills up nearly every evening. For kids, El Borne has an immense zoo and a chocolate museum, both of which can hardly be considered punishment for parents. Art lovers definitely have to head for the Museu Picasso, a place that can't afford to be missed!

6 Musts!

Parc de la Ciutadella

A stroll around
Parc de la Ciutadella.

Pucca

Lunch at Pucca.

Museu Picasso

Daydreaming at the
Picasso Museum.

Custo

An authentic
Custo t-shirt.

La Vinya del Senyor

A tipple of wine at
La Vinya del Senyor.

1748

Spanish pottery as a gift
(and for yourself!).

⭕ **Sights**
⭕ **Shopping**

🔘 **Food & drink**
⭕ **Nice to do**

Sights

① Thanks to the 1988 World's Fair, there's a little piece of Paris right here in Barcelona. This **Arc de Triomf** is more Right Bank than Barcelona, but it's still imposing. It was designed by the architect Josep Vilaseca. *passeig de lluis companys, metro arc de triomf*

② **Palau de Justicia** is located to the left of the Arc de Triomf. This big, modern construction was built in 1915, largely by Sagnier. A court of law is something you don't want to get too intimate with, so a view from the outside is more than enough. *passeig de lluis companys, metro arc de triomf*

③ You can see covered market halls throughout the whole city, and yet **Mercat de Santa Caterina** is worth visiting. Take in the atmosphere and buy a tasty piece of fruit for later. Or, as many Spaniards do: a piece of dried tuna.

passeig de lluis companys, open mon-wed, fri-sat 8am-2.30pm and 5pm-8pm, thu 8am-8.30pm, metro arc de triomf

⑤ The **Museu de Zoologia** looks like a castle, complete with a tower. Inside, you'll find an enormous collection of stuffed animals (by taxidermists, not Mattel) and skeletons of prehistoric creatures.

parc de la ciutadella s/n, telephone 93 319 69 12, open tue-sun 10am-2pm (thu until 6.30pm), admission €3, including admission to the museu de geologia, metro arc de triomf

⑦ In the same park, you'll also find the small **Museu de Geologia**, where you can find out everything about fossils. Interesting for geology buffs.

parc de la ciutadella s/n, telephone 93 319 68 95, open tue-sun 10am-2pm (thu until 6.30pm), admission €3, including admission to the museu de zoologia, metro arc de triomf

⑬ A more accessible subject for a museum is chocolate! In the **Museu de la Xocolata**, chocolate lovers learn that the stuff is good for your health. Thank God! Also find out about the origins of chocolate and view some fascinating, mouthwatering sculptures. There's also a small shop where you can buy some chocolate.

antiguo de san agustin comerç 36, telephone 93 268 78 78, open mon-sat 10am-7pm, sun and holidays 10am-3pm, admission €3, metro arc de triomf

㉓ The **Palau Dalmases** was built in the 15th century. The beautiful staircase near the entrance on the small square is especially appealing. Even nicer is the café on the ground floor, with its wonderful baroque interior. Order a 'copa de cava', a glass of Spanish champagne. And, if you're lucky, there's even live music.

c. de montcada 20, telephone 93 310 06 73, open tue-sat 8pm-2am, sun 6pm-10pm., metro jaume l

museu de la xocolata

FUNDACIÓ PRIVADA DE L'ESCOLA DEL GREMI DE PASTISSERIA I MUSEU DE LA XOCOLATA DE BARCELONA

(13) MUSEU DE LA XOCOLATA

(25) The **Museu Picasso** is an essential stop when visiting Barcelona, especially since Picasso was born in the city. The most extensive collection by this influential artist is on display here. Aside from artworks ranging from Picasso's early years to his Blue and Pink Periods, you'll also be able to view temporary exhibitions.

c. de montcada 15-23, telephone 93 319 63 10, open tue-sat 10am-8pm, sun 10am-3pm, admission €4.80, metro jaume I

(26) Centuries-old pre-Colombian art is exhibited in the small **Museu Barbier-Mueller d'Art precolombi**. You'll see ceramics, sculptures, jewels and textiles made by the Aztecs, Mayas and Incas. This is one of the few museums that also organizes workshops.

c. de montcada 12-14, telephone 93 310 45 16, open tue-sat 10am-6pm, sun and holidays 10am-3pm, admission €3, including admission to the museu tèxtil i d'indumentària, metro jaume I

(27) The **Museu Tèxtil i d'Indumentària**, or the Textile Museum, has a collection of around 4,000 pieces. It's full of beautiful clothing items and accessories from the 4th - 20th century. After you're done looking around, grab a bite or have a drink on the adjoining terrace.

c. de montcada 12-14, telephone 93 310 45 16, open tue-sat 10am-6pm, sun and holidays 10am-3pm, admission €3.50, including admission to the museu de barbier-mueller, café open daily 10am-midnight, telephone 93 368 25 98, metro jaume I

(31) **Santa Maria del Mar** is the church in the center of El Borne, and it's known to be one of the most beautiful churches in Barcelona. If you're lucky, you'll be able to witness a Spanish wedding ceremony. Talk about a feast for the eyes!

plaça de santa maria, open daily 9am-1.30pm and 4.30pm-8pm, metro jaume I

Food & drink

(8) **Hivernacle** is a great spot for recuperation. Rest on their ideal terrace. Admire the covered garden. Also check out the listings of jazz concerts, as they're really good.
passeig de picasso, telephone 93 295 40 17, open daily 2pm-4pm and 8pm-1am, metro arc de triomf

(9) **El Foro** has a very extensive menu, and you can make your choice from a selection ranging from fish to meat, from a hint of Argentinean to a touch of Italian cuisine. The restaurant has a cozy atmosphere, and they even have a house photographer who'll take your picture and develop it while you're eating. Recently, El Foro has added a club in the basement, where you can have a nice chat and put on your dancing shoes after dinner.
c. de la princesa 53, telephone 93 310 10 20, open mon-thu 1pm-4pm and 9pm-midnight, fri-sat 1pm-4pm and 9pm-12.30am, entrance price €7, metro jaume I

(10) **Gente de Pasta** is 100% Italian in a modern setting. The interior is trendy, with bright colors on the wall, and a DJ spins quiet background music. And the food? Typically Italian, from carpaccio to delectable salads with parmesan cheese, from pizza to pasta. If you like spicy food, the pasta with peppers is recommended! And you'll be able to sit and enjoy your meal without being rushed out the door.
passeig de picasso 10, telephone 93 268 70 17, open daily 1pm-4pm and 9pm-12.30am, menu price €8.50, metro arc de triomf

(11) **Taira** is a Japanese restaurant with a modern but cozy interior. And the food is delicious: steamed vegetables, large bowls of noodles, good sushi… Enjoy it all.
c. del comerç 7, telephone 93 310 24 97, open tue-sun noon-4pm and 9pm-12.30am, menu price €10, metro arc de triomf

HIVERNACLE (8)

⑭ **SANDWICH & FRIENDS**

⑫ **Pucca** is hip and happening in El Borne, and the inhabitants are quite happy about it. It's a small restaurant, simply decorated, with a fantastic menu. Make sure that you're hungry, as the plates are well filled.
passeig de picasso 32, telephone 93 268 72 36, open tue-thu noon-2am, fri-sat noon-3am, menu price €9, metro arc de triomf

⑭ Nice variations at **Sandwich & Friends**. Here they serve a sort of rolled-up grilled ham and cheese sandwich with the tastiest filling imaginable. With a little luck, you'll be able to grab a seat on the terrace and be kept amused by street entertainers while you eat.
passeig del born, telephone 93 310 07 86, open sun-wed 11am-12.30am, thu-sat 11am-1am, price €4, metro jaume I

⑮ **La Taverna del Born** also has a wonderful terrace where you can enjoy tapas in all shapes and sizes. Add an order of 'pan con tomate'. These pieces of French bread, spread with olive oil and the flesh of the tomato, are especially delicious here. In addition to this, there's a large variety of meat, fish and vegetarian tapas.
passeig del born 27-29, telephone 93 315 09 64, open tue-sat 11am-midnight (wed until 12.30am, fri-sat until 1am), sun 11am-5pm, metro jaume I

⑲ Quiet simplicity: that's **Salero**! A restaurant that's getting a lot of good reviews, and rightly so! Salero has a small but delicious menu. The predominantly white décor is especially attractive. Need we add that you really need to reserve here?
c. del rec 60, telephone 93 319 80 22, open mon-wed 1.30pm-4pm and 9pm-midnight, thu-sat 1.30pm-4pm and from 9pm onwards, price €11, metro jaume I

㉑ **Cal Pep** is a famous fish restaurant in El Borne. It's a small, narrow place, and it could be that everyone standing at the bar is waiting for one of the few little tables. However, you can also order amazing calamari, grilled gambas, and other dishes at the bar.
pl. de les olles 8, telephone 93 310 79 61, open mon 8pm-midnight, tue-sat 1.15pm-4.15pm and 8pm-midnight, price €10, metro jaume I

㉙ **El Pebre Blau** is one of two restaurants facing each other in this street. This is the newer, more modern version of the one across the street. Attractive, colorful walls with long hanging lamps and a wonderful mix of Italian, Oriental and Catalan cuisine on the menu.
c. dels banys vells, telephone 93 319 13 08, open daily from 9 onwards, price €12, metro jaume I

㉜ If you want to kick back for a bit with a glass of wine, **La Vinya del Senyor** is the place to be. Relax in style on the small square near the church, and immerse yourself in the cozy atmosphere of this neighborhood. It's guaranteed that you'll be served good wine or cava.
plaça de santa maria 5, telephone 93 310 33 70, open noon-1am, metro jaume I

㉟ **La Carassa** must be ancient, or so it seems. Entering through a very small door, you arrive in a tiny restaurant filled from top to bottom with bric-a-brac. However, the fondue is fantastic, and you can be proud of yourself if you're able to eat everything. As a nice touch, the ladies receive a lovely red flower when you leave. Less nice is the necessity of washing your clothes as soon as you get home to get the smell out.
c. brosoli 1, telephone 93 310 33 06, open mon-sat 9pm-11pm (kitchen), fondue price from €20, metro jaume I

Shopping

(16) **Kwatra** is new, beautiful and exclusive, and you can choose from the trendiest Nikes offered at the moment. Owner Robbie, always eager to chat, does his best to keep his customers satisfied. Not only the newest sneakers, but also a very hip line of clothing.
c. antic de sant joan 1, telephone 93 268 08 04, open mon-sat 10.30am-8.30pm, metro jaume I

(17) **Onno** has a very nice collection of clothing for both men and women. Here, you'll be able to leave with an affordable item and steal the show for the rest of the year when wearing it. Don't be surprised if you have to ring the bell to get in. That's normal here.
c. de la ribera 1, telephone 93 319 54 77, open mon-sat 11am-9pm, metro jaume I

(18) A hip store for men: that's **Carhartt**. Founded in Michigan in 1889, Carhartt now has several locations throughout Europe, and one of them is in Barcelona. A lot of shirts in different colors, comfy jackets and cool jeans. There's also a ladies' collection, but it's fairly limited.
c. del rec 75, telephone 93 319 63 47, open mon-fri 11am-2.30pm and 4pm-8.30pm, sat 11am-8.30pm, metro jaume I

(20) 'Hot' in Barcelona means wearing t-shirts by **Custo**. They're certainly not cheap, but every shirt is a colorful work of art in itself, ensuring you steal the show. And that costs a bit of money. At least go in and see what everyone's raving about.
plaça de les olles 7, telephone 93 268 78 93, open mon-sat 10am-10pm, sun 1pm-8pm, metro jaume I

(22) You can get the best souvenirs at **1748**. You'll find all sorts of colorful pottery, from bowls to plates, vases, olive dishes… Your kitchen at home will soon have that Spanish touch. The pleasant owner will also thoroughly wrap everything for you, so you can board the airplane without worrying.
placeta de montcada 2, telephone 93 319 54 13, open mon-sat 10.30am-2.30pm and 4.30pm-8pm, metro jaume I

㉔ **0,925** is full of handmade jewelry, and each piece is prettier than the next. If you're looking for a small bauble, chances are you'll find it here.
c. de montcada 25, telephone 93 319 43 18, open mon-fri 10.30am-8.30pm, sat 11am-8pm, sun 11.30am-3.30pm, metro jaume I

㉘ The owner of **Ninets** opened her store in early 2002. She sells small baby rompers and other clothing for infants, all with an added touch in the form of a hand-painted flower, bear or cow. And, if you like, she'll even make your purchase more personal by adding baby's name. This place makes new mothers happy.
c. dels banys vells 19, telephone 93 268 19 09, open mon 5.30pm-8pm, tue-sat 10.30am-2pm and 5.30pm-8pm, metro jaume I

㉚ **E&A Gispert** has been here since 1851. The shop's not hard to find: just follow your nose. Home-roasted almonds and many other sorts of nuts, Spanish turron (a kind of nougat) and the most delicious sun-dried tomatoes... You can buy them all here. Just like everybody else in El Borne does.
c. dels sombrerers 23, telephone 93 319 75 35, open mon-fri 9am-1.30pm and 4pm-7.30pm, sat 10am-2pm and 5pm-8pm (open 9.30am in aug), metro jaume I

㉝ What don't they have at **Vientos del Sur**? This is one of those great shops where you can browse around for stuff you don't really need, stuff that's nice to own all the same: slippers, jewelry, candles, clothing and other must-haves.
c. de l'argenteria 78, telephone 93 268 25 25, open daily 11am-9pm, metro jaume I

㉞ **Kwaleon** sells clothing, shoes and matching accessories. This is a very small, amusing shop, and every inch is covered with stuff. The owner, Jack, sells clothing by brands such as Dolce & Gabbana, Gucci and Diesel.
c. de manresa 8 (corner of c. de l'argenteria), telephone 93 268 39 39, open mon-sat 10am-9pm, three sun a month noon-8pm, metro jaume I

④ PARC DE LA CIUTADELLA

Nice to do

(4) **Parc de la Ciutadella** is big, and there's always something to do. You can take a nice walk or rest on one of the many benches or in the grass under the trees. Spot tiny parrots. There's an impressive monument in the park, near the pond, where you can feed the ducks and hire a boat. On Sundays, all sorts of people with musical instruments gather to make music. Everybody dances, drinks and enjoys the weather.
metro barceloneta or ciutadella-vila olímpica

(6) Barcelona's **Parc Zoològic Acuarama**, the zoo, is great! It's very well maintained, and the animals' natural habitats have been recreated with attention to detail. The most popular attraction is 'copito de nieve', a large, albino gorilla who goes by the name of Snowflake. There's also a dolphin show several times a day. Make sure you're there on time, especially on warm days, because your morning is over before you know it.
parc de la ciutadella, telephone 93 225 67 80, open daily 10am7.30pm (until 5pm during the winter), entrance €10, metro arc de triomf

El Borne

WALKING TOUR 5

Cross the road at metro Arc de Triomf, and walk through the Arc de Triomf (1), passing the Palau de Justicia (2) and the Mercat de Santa Caterina (3), heading in the direction of Parc de la Ciutadella (4). When you enter the park, the Museu de Zoologia (5) is on your right. You can take a nice stroll in the direction of the zoo (6), the monument, the pond, or the Museu de Geologia (7). Cross the street via Hivernacle (8), and enter the c. de la Princesa. On the corner and further down, you'll find several good restaurants for lunch (9) (10) (11) (12). Just to the right, on the c. del Comerç, is the Chocolate Museum (13). Back on the c. del Comerç, walk in the direction of the Mercat del Born for a few nice terraces (14) (15). To the left, in the c. Antic de Sant Joan, you'll find Kwatra (16) on your right and, further down and around the corner, Onno (17). Via the side street, with Carhartt (18) on the corner, enter the c. del Rec. Salero (19) is on your left. Walking via c. del Bonaire, you'll bump into the Custo store (20). On the left side of the square, you'll find a wonderful fish restaurant (21). Walk back to the right, via Plaça de les Olles, to the Passeig del Born. Cross the street, entering the Plaçeta de Montcada. On your left is the pottery shop (22), and further down you'll find the Palau Dalmases with café (23), a nice jeweler (24), but also the Museu Picasso (25), Museu Barbier-Mueller (26), and the Museu Tèxtil i d'Indumetària with its cozy café (27). Take a left into c. de la Barra de Ferro, and get lost in the labyrinth of small streets full of small shops and restaurants (28) (29). Keep on walking, via c. dels Banys Vells, until you reach the rear of the church. Before you walk to the right, you'll find Gispert (30) around the corner to your left. On the square in front of the church Santa Maria del Mar (31), you can stop for a glass of wine at Vinya del Senyor (32). Do some more shopping or look for a good restaurant by following the road upwards, into the c. de l'Argenteria (33) (34) (35).

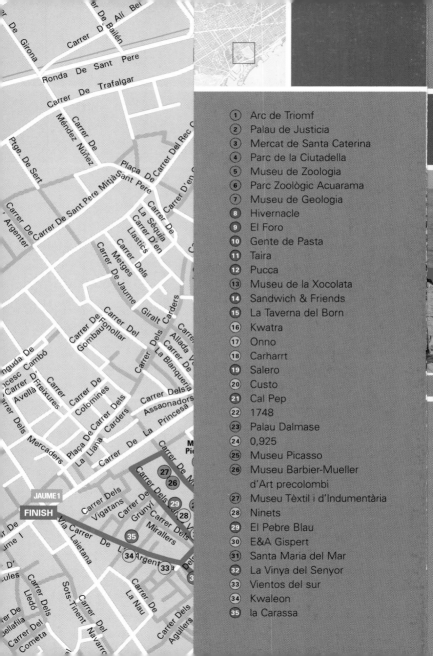

1. Arc de Triomf
2. Palau de Justicia
3. Mercat de Santa Caterina
4. Parc de la Ciutadella
5. Museu de Zoologia
6. Parc Zoològic Acuarama
7. Museu de Geologia
8. Hivernacle
9. El Foro
10. Gente de Pasta
11. Taira
12. Pucca
13. Museu de la Xocolata
14. Sandwich & Friends
15. La Taverna del Born
16. Kwatra
17. Onno
18. Carharrt
19. Salero
20. Custo
21. Cal Pep
22. 1748
23. Palau Dalmase
24. 0,925
25. Museu Picasso
26. Museu Barbier-Mueller d'Art precolombi
27. Museu Tèxtil i d'Indumentària
28. Ninets
29. El Pebre Blau
30. E&A Gispert
31. Santa Maria del Mar
32. La Vinya del Senyor
33. Vientos del sur
34. Kwaleon
35. la Carassa

6 Musts!

Museu d'Història de Catalunya

Take a look at Catalonia's historical museum.

Luz de Gas

Eat lunch on the Luz de Gas boat.

l'Aquarium

Visit L'Aquarium's underwater world.

Teleféric

Enjoy the view from the cable cars.

Boulevard

Stroll in style on the boulevard.

Oven

Make a detour, and eat dinner at Oven.

○ **Sights**

○ **Shopping**

● **Food & drink**

○ **Nice to do**

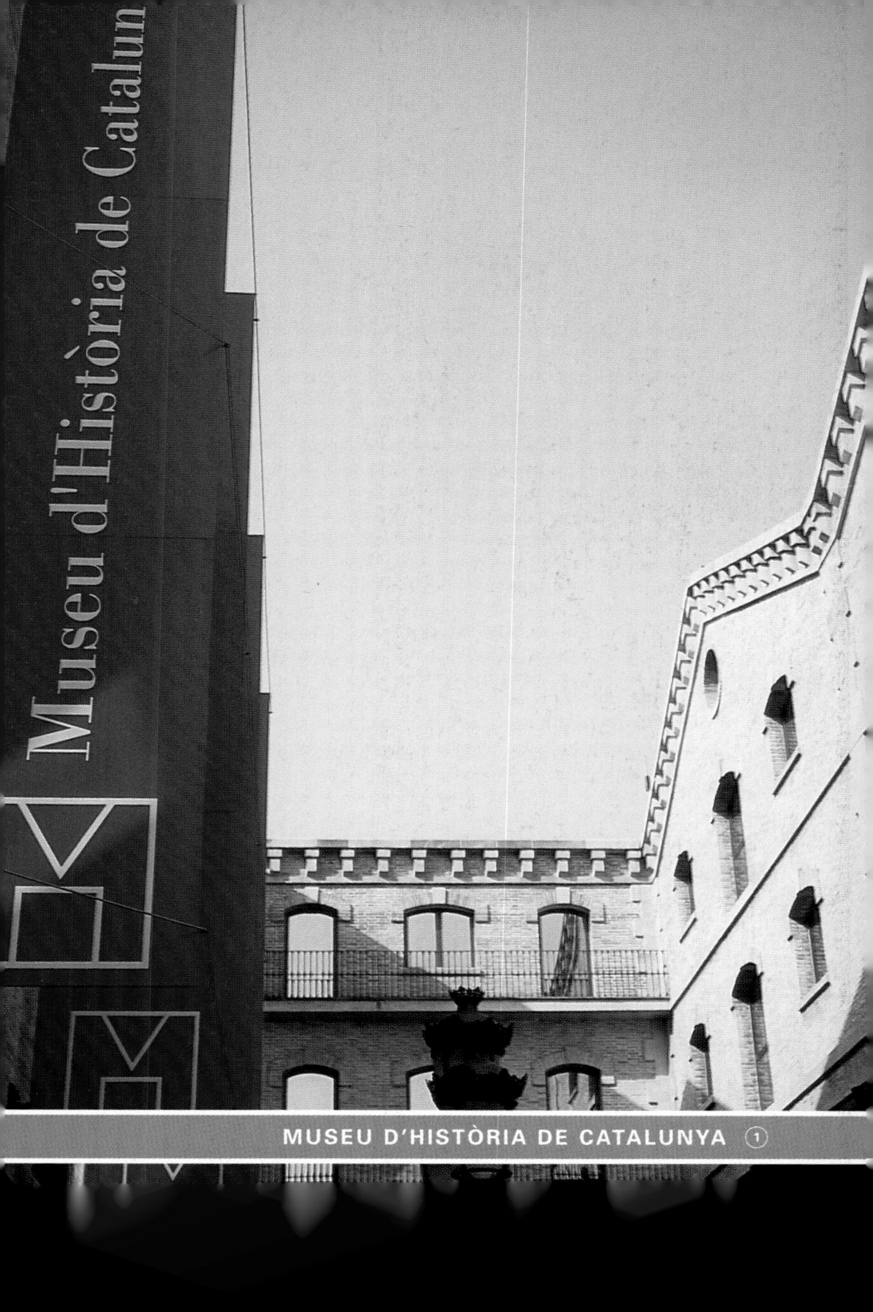

MUSEU D'HISTÒRIA DE CATALUNYA ①

Sights

(1) The transparent entrance to the **Museu d'Història de Catalunya** is extremely impressive. Find out everything about Catalonia's 2,000-year-old history, from the Paleolithic Era up to recent political events. The building used to be a warehouse until it was converted into a museum in 1990.
plaça pau vila 3, telephone 93 225 47 00, open wed 10am-8pm, thu-sat 10am-7pm, sun and holidays 10am-2.30pm, admission €3, http://cultura.gencat.es/museus/mhc, metro barceloneta

(7) This **statue of Columbus** was erected in the 19th century and commemorates the explorer's return to Barcelona after discovering the New World in 1492. His finger, at a height of about 60 yards, points to the sea. It's possible to take an elevator to the top in order to enjoy the spectacular view.
portal de la pau z/n, open daily 9am-8.30pm, admission €1.80, metro drassanes

(10) You'll find the **Museu Maritim** just down the road. This is where the Drassanes, the royal shipyards, used to be. Nowadays, the location is home to an extensive maritime museum, and you can admire a large collection of ships. Even if you're not exactly a boat lover, you'll have to admit that this amazing gothic building, with its accompanying terrace, is worth the visit alone.
av. drassanes s/n, telephone 93 342 99 20, open daily 10am-7pm, admission €5.40, www.diba.es/mmaritim, metro drassanes

⑬ This idyllic little square in the heart of **Barceloneta** is home to the Church of Sant Miguel, built between 1753 and 1863. Local inhabitants always find something to celebrate here on religious holidays. Whether it be in the form of a parade or a fireworks display, you can bet that the whole neighborhood will be there.

plaça de la barceloneta, metro barceloneta

⑭ Having arrived at the giant whale, you'll find yourself in **Vila Olímpica**. Next to the whale are two towers, both over 150 yards tall. One of the towers houses the famous Hotel Arts, while the other, the Torre Mapfre, is filled with luxury offices. Vila Olímpica was built to provide accommodations for 1992's Olympic athletes. The buildings' worldly atmosphere and modern style stand in stark contrast to Barceloneta's small and narrow streets. Every Sunday is a true event here as Spaniards parade down the boulevard, eyeing vendors and their wares at the myriad of stalls. Later on in the day, you'll find everyone at the fish restaurants and little bars near the harbor.

vila olímpica, metro ciutadella-vila olímpica

Food & drink

(2) What could be more wonderful than sitting outside, enjoying a view of the harbor, with a plate full of fresh seafood in front of you? Experience all of this at **Merendero de la Mari**. From calamari to scampi, lobster to the famous arroz negro (black rice)… If you love to eat seafood, don't miss this place.
plaça pau vila 1, telephone 93 221 31 41, open mon-sat 12.30pm-4pm and 8.30pm-11.30pm, sun 12.30pm-4pm, price €15, metro barceloneta

(3) Life is very, very sweet on the boat **Luz de Gas**. Recline upstairs on the deck with a view of the water, a glass of rosé and some delicious tapas, and sing along with the music. If you feel like putting on your boogie shoes, stay in your seat until the evening, when the dance floor on the wharf opens up.
moll del dipòsit, open daily 12am-3am, price €3.50, metro barceloneta

(6) Everything's a touch on the ritzy side at **Reial Club Marítim de Barcelona**, including the terrace overlooking the harbor. If you feel like devouring an upscale meal, you won't be disappointed here!
moll d'espanya s/n (front of maremagnum), telephone 93 221 62 56, open daily 1.30pm-4pm and 9pm-11.30pm, price €15, metro drassanes

(12) **Ruccula** was recently renovated, and its style now leans toward contemporary design. The inside boasts a minimalist interior where you'll enjoy a pleasant view of the harbor. If you sit outside, you'll be amused by the show the fountain puts on for you.
moll de barcelona, telephone 93 508 82 68, open mon-sat 9am-4pm and 8.30pm-midnight, sandwich price €3, metro drassanes

(17) One of the nice things about **Agua** is that you practically end up eating dinner right on the beach. The restaurant has a Mediterranean kitchen, and you can choose from a variety of tasty tapas as a starter. The interior is trendy but cozy. The art on the wall is original, the waiters are friendly, and the sun sets right in front of you. What else could you possibly want?
passeig marítim de la barceloneta 30, telephone 93 225 12 72, open mon-sat 1pm-4pm and 8.30pm-11.30pm, sun 1pm-4pm, price €12, metro ciutadella-vila olímpica

(18) The nice thing about Irish pubs is the friendly atmosphere you'll always find therein. That's definitely the case at **Kennedy**. This is a great place to have a chat with authentic Spanish, British and Irish people, as well as with the folks who've docked their boat in the harbor and, heck, anyone else in the mood for a good pint of Guiness and live music.
moll mestral 26-27, telephone 93 221 00 39, open mon-fri 6pm-3.30am,
sat 5pm-4.30am, sun 4pm-3.30am, www.kennedyirishpub.com,
metro ciutadella-vila olímpica

(20) **Base Nautica** is one of the nicest beach bars in Barcelona. The place is a little further away from the harbor and therefore a little further away from the throngs of tourists. This is a nice spot to grab a bite or have a drink while sunbathing on your towel. A DJ provides summery vibes.
playa de la marbella, open daily 11am-midnight, tapas price €3,
metro ciutadella-vila olímpica

(23) One of Barcelona's newest hotspots is **Oven**, a great combination of lounge bar, nightclub and restaurant. It's not too close to the harbor, but once you're there you won't want to leave. Have a pre-dinner cocktail in the lounge, and then move on to the restaurant where you can choose from a surprisingly diverse menu. During the weekend, everything's moved to the side, and partygoers dance until the wee hours of the morning.
c. de ramon turró 126, telephone 93 221 06 02, open mon-thu, sun 9pm-
2am, fri-sat 9pm-3am, price €12, metro ciutadella-vila olímpica

④ **MAREMAGNUM**

Shopping

(4) **Maremagnum** is a diverse complex. It's a shopping mall with restaurants, a movie theater and several clubs. Especially handy if you still need to buy some flip-flops, a bikini or sunglasses on your way to the beach. Walk into sportswear store Rabent and knick-knack shop WAE. Don't bother eating at the mall. There are many other places both better and cheaper.
plaça de maremagnum 2, moll d'espanya s/n, telephone 93 225 81 00, metro barceloneta or drassanes

(9) There's a small antique market every Saturday and Sunday from 8am to 8pm on the **Plaça Portal de la Pau**, next to the statue of Columbus. You'll find about 20 stalls full of jewelry, prints and pottery. If you look closely, you're sure to find something worth your while.
plaça portal de la pau, open sat-sun 8am-8pm, metro drassanes

WORLD TRADE CENTER

Nice to do

(5) To discover the wild world of underwater life, be sure to visit **L'Aquarium**, one of the largest aquariums in Europe. Not only will you see hundreds of different fish, but they also have penguins, and you can even pet rays. Lots of fun for the kids, and it's educational!
maremagnum, telephone 93 221 74 74, open daily sep-jun 9.30am-9pm, jul-aug 9.30am-11pm, price €11, metro barceloneta

(8) If you feel like spending some time in the water, take a boat trip with **Golondrinas**. Their excursions range from half an hour through the harbor to one-and-a-half hours heading towards Port Olímpico. Drink in a true sea breeze. Be sure to ask when the departure times are, as they tend to vary due to the weather.
moll de les drassanes, telephone 93 442 31 06, open daily, price €8, metro drassanes

(11) Feel like taking the **Teleféric**, the cable car up to Montjuïc? Definitely do, as the view from the mountain is very impressive, especially if you travel all the way to the Museu Militar de Montjuïc at the top.
teleféric, open daily oct-may 11am-7.15pm, jun-sep 11am-9pm, price €4.50, metro drassanes

(15) Ready for a sauna, massage, algae wrap or a yoga lesson? This **Marítim Poliesportiu** (health center) offers many opportunities for you to totally unwind. The basic fee is good for three hours of unencumbered relaxation. The building's entrance is located to the right of the hospital, and the complex itself is completely underground. You need to reserve in advance for special treatments, but be aware that not everyone here speaks English.
marítim poliesportiu, passeig marítim 33-35, telephone 93 224 04 40, open mon-fri 7am-midnight, sat 8am-9pm, sun 8am-5pm, price mon-fri €11.50, sat-sun €14 for three hours, www.claror.org, metro ciutadella-vila olímpica

⑯ Feel like pedaling around? Rent a 'yellow bike' at **Biciclot** on the beach. You can even take a special tour through the city on Friday evenings from 10pm to midnight and from 11am to 1pm during the weekend. At least you'll able to say that you were active during your vacation…
passeig marítim 33-35, telephone 93 221 97 78, open apr-sep daily 10am-7pm, oct-mar fri-sun and holidays 10am-7pm, www.biciclot.net, metro ciutadella-vila olímpica

⑲ For those wanting to take a chance or who are clamoring for a touch of glamour, look no further than the **Gran Casino de Barcelona**. Put on your Sunday best, and go out and try your luck. If you're not so fortunate, there are still several bars, restaurants and a disco you can visit - if you've got some spare change.
c. de la marina 19-21, telephone 93 225 78 78, open daily 1pm-5am, admission €4.50, metro ciutadella-vila olímpica

㉑ You can hire your own boat at **Geomar**, from classic yachts to motorboats and sailboats. For one day or for your whole vacation.
port olímpico, muelle marina 4802, telephone 93 221 39 24, www.geomarnautica.com, metro ciutadella-vila olímpica

㉒ The **Cineplex** theater has 15 screens, and it's also one of the few cinemas to show movies in their original languages. You can catch the latest releases every day, starting in the morning. Everything has Spanish subtitles, so if you want to learn the language, read along.
c. de salvador espriu 61, downstairs in centre comercial, telephone 93 221 75 85, open daily 11:30am-1am, price mon 4, tue-sun €5.50, metro ciutadella-vila olímpica

PORT OLÍMPICO

Barceloneta & Vila Olímpica

At metro station Barceloneta, cross the street to find the Catalonian Historical Museum ①. To the left, you can choose from a variety of seafood restaurants ② or lunch or dine on the Luz de Gas boat ③, enjoying a view of the Port Vell harbor. From Luz de Gas, take a left in the direction of Maremagnum ④. On your left is one of the world's largest aquariums ⑤. If you're still contemplating food, there is a restaurant onshore that's perfect for that special occasion ⑥. Walk in the direction of Columbus ⑦, crossing the wave-like bridge. This is where you'll find a small antique market on Saturdays and Sundays ⑨. If you feel like taking a boat trip, head for the Golondrinas ⑧. If you keep walking towards the north, you'll arrive at the Museu Marítim ⑩. Continue your walk, via the museum, towards the Teleféric ⑪ and the World Trade Center. Feel like resting a bit? Drop by one of the many sidewalk cafés here ⑫. Take the cable car to Barceloneta ⑬, and walk in the direction of the beach. If you don't want to take the cable car, walk back towards the historical museum, and walk to the left of the boats until you arrive at Barceloneta's beach. Stroll on the boulevard until you reach the shiny whale ⑭, which you should be able to see from afar. Discover Barceloneta and its tiny square and church. To the right of the hospital is where the sauna is ⑮. This is the perfect place to recoup some of your energy. Sports enthusiasts can hire a bicycle at the beach ⑯. You'll also find lots of restaurants and bars next to each other ⑰ ⑱. Walk underneath the whale, past the casino ⑲, heading towards the boulevard at Port Olimpico's harbor ⑳ ㉑. Here, you can spend the whole evening at one of the nice restaurants ㉓, bars or at the movie theater ㉒.

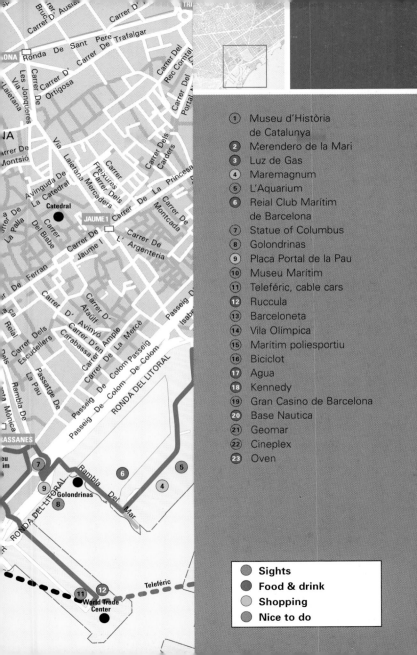

1. Museu d'Història de Catalunya
2. Merendero de la Mari
3. Luz de Gas
4. Maremagnum
5. L'Aquarium
6. Reial Club Marítim de Barcelona
7. Statue of Columbus
8. Golondrinas
9. Placa Portal de la Pau
10. Museu Marítim
11. Teleféric, cable cars
12. Ruccula
13. Barceloneta
14. Vila Olímpica
15. Marítim poliesportiu
16. Biciclot
17. Agua
18. Kennedy
19. Gran Casino de Barcelona
20. Base Nautica
21. Geomar
22. Cineplex
23. Oven

● **Sights**
● **Food & drink**
● **Shopping**
● **Nice to do**

Sights outside of the city center

If you follow the walking routes in this guide, you'll pass by almost all of Barcelona's main attractions. However, there are still a few spots worth visiting away from the city center. You can reach them by bus or metro, but also sometimes by taking the Bus Turistic.

(K) One of the attractions is **Montjuïc**. You can take wonderful walks through the park on this mountain, as well as visit fountains and museums. You can get there by bus or metro, or by taking the cable car, which departs at the World Trade Center or a bit further down on Barceloneta's beach. However, you can also follow Bus Turistic's blue route, stopping at every attraction. This way, you'll also get a detailed description of the sights, and you'll receive a coupon booklet, entitling you to discounts at various museums.

(L) The **Museu Nacional d'Art de Catalunya** lies at the edge of Montjuïc; you can even see the building from the Plaça d'Espanya. This impressive building looks like a castle, and you should really take a look inside. You'll find all of the most important works of Roman art on display.
palau nacional, telephone 93 622 03 75, www.mnac.es, open tue-sat 10am-7pm, sun and holidays 10am-2.30pm, admission €3.60, metro espanya, bus 50, bus turistic blue route

(M) There are gigantic **fountains** in front of the Museu Nacional d'Art de Catalunya, and they are especially worth seeing in the evening, when, by making use of lighting effects, the fountains seem to be spraying water in a multitude of colors. The accompanying music makes it all absolutely breathtaking, most notably when you hear Freddie Mercury singing 'Barcelona', the official song of the 1992 Summer Olympics.
palau nacional, jun-sep thu-sun 9.30pm-11.30pm (15-minute intervals), oct-may fri-sat 7pm-9pm, admission free, metro espanya, bus 50, bus turistic blue route

PORT VELL

(N) You'll find the **Joan Miró** museum, among other things, in the Parc de Montjuïc. Here you can see the painter's works, from 1914 to 1978.
parc de montjuïc s/n, telephone 93 443 94 70, www.bcn.fjmiro.es, open oct-jun tue-wed, fri-sat 10am-7pm, thu 10am-9.30pm, sun and holidays 10am-2.30pm, jul-sep tue-wed, fri-sat 10am-8pm, thu 10am-9.30pm, sun and holidays 10am-2.30pm, admission €7.20, bus 50, bus turistic blue route

(O) Location-wise, **Museu Militar de Montjuïc** is one of the most beautiful museums in Barcelona. Inside, you'll find an enormous collection of weapons, maps and an assortment of military items.
castell de montjuïc, telephone 93 329 86 13, open nov-mar tue-sun 9.30am-4.30pm, apr-oct tue-sun 9.30am-7.30pm, admission €2.40, bus 50, bus turistic blue route to teleferic (cable cars)

(P) All the way on the other side of the city is where you'll find
FC Barcelona's stadium, also known as **Camp Nou**. You can explore the soccer museum and also the actual playing field. If you're lucky, you'll bump into one of the players, and if not, your trip still won't have been for nothing. The museum is certainly recommended for all soccer fans, and you can buy game tickets from the cashier, just in case you want to catch a soccer match.
arístides maillol, entrance 7 or 9, telephone 93 496 36 00, www.fcbarcelona.es, open mon-sat 10am-6.30pm, sun and holidays 10am-2pm, admission €3.50, metro collblanc, bus turistic red route

Nightlife

Barcelona sparkles, especially at night. Countless clubs are spread all over town. Prepare for sizzling nights on a daily basis.

(Q) You'll find several nightclubs perfect for dancing the night away on Montjuïc, near **Poble Espanyol**. One of them is La Terrazza, one of Barcelona's trendiest hot spots. Drag queens and dancers join you under the stars and in between the palm trees at this outdoor club.
avinguda marquès de comillas, telephone 93 423 12 85,
open fri-sat midnight-6am, metro espanya

(R) **Torres de Ávila** is also on Montjuïc. This club, with its intimate corners and many bars, plays host to the most influential Spanish DJs. Be sure to take your drink upstairs to the outdoor terrace for a magnificent view of the city.
avenguda marquès de comillas s/n, telephone 93 424 93 09,
www.viptorresdeavila.com, open fri-sat midnight-6.30am, metro espanya

(S) This used to be a wonderful ballroom where couples would practice the cha-cha-cha. Nowadays, **La Paloma** is very popular with Barcelona's in-crowd. Depending on the evening, you'll hear everything from techno to old-school disco, all in a breathtaking interior.
c. tigre 27, telephone 93 301 68 97, open thu 6pm-9.30pm and 11.30pm-3am, fri-sat 6pm-9.30pm and 11.30pm-5.30am, sun 6pm-10pm,
metro sant antoni or universitat

(T) If you love funk or soul music, **Café Royale** is the place to be. Swing away in the main room or chill with a cocktail in the lounge, reclining in one of the comfortable armchairs.
c. nou de zurbano 3, telephone 93 317 61 24, open mon-thu 5pm-2.30am, fri-sat 5pm-3am, metro drassanes or liceu

X OVEN

(U) **Danzatoria** has to be up there on the list of hot spots. This is a club with different themed rooms and a terrace with a view. DJs spin pop, house and ambient in this establishment on Mount Tibidabo.
avenguda tibidabo 61, torre 1, telephone 93 268 74 30, open thu-sat 11pm-3am, sun 6pm-2.30am, metro penitents

(V) You'll find a whole row of nightclubs and bars along **Port Olímpico**. The musical styles vary from Latin to popular, house to techno, and you'll find women dancing on the bars almost everywhere. Luckily, there's a nice Irish pub among some of these sleezy clubs, and you'll be able to hear some good live music there on the weekends.
port olímpico, metro ciutadella-vila olímpica

(W) At around midnight, the restaurant **Salsitas** transforms into **Club 22**. All of the tables are moved out, and what remains is a large dance floor filled with gyrating - and often beautiful - people. The atmosphere is always good here. Should you overheat while boogying away, there's the possibility of taking a breather in the lounge, with the help of a refreshing cocktail. A DJ will provide back-up for you, spinning mellow grooves.
c. nou de la rambla 22, telephone 93 318 08 40, open fri-sat midnight-5am, metro liceu

(X) After enjoying a delicious dinner at **Oven**, grab your drink and take a seat on one of the large red sofas in the front of the restaurant. Once you're inside the place, you won't want to leave anymore. DJs ensure that the music puts you in the mood for dancing. Oven is popular with a very mixed crowd.
c. de ramon turró 126, telephone 93 221 06 02, open mon-wed, sun 9pm-2am, fri-sat 9pm-3am, metro ciutadella-vila olímpica

Alphabetical index

0,925	110
1748	109

a

agua	125
antic hospital santa creu	93
antoni tàpies foundation	43
aquarium, l'	131
arc de triomf	99
armand basi	51

b

b.huno	91
bar amsterdam	44
bar kastola	26
bar terra	26
barceloneta	116-133
base nautica	126
biciclot	132
bilbao-berria	63
borne, el	96-115
buenas migas	63
bulevard rosa	51
bus turístic	18

c

cachitos	44
caelumis	70
cafè de l'acadèmia	63
café del sol	29
café royale	139
café shilling	67
caffe di roma, il	46
cal pep	107

camp nou	138
cantina machito	26
caracoles, los	67
carassa, la	108
carhartt	109
casa battló	43
casa del libre	48
casa milà	43
casa miranda martì	70
casa vincens	25
casas	73
cccb	80
centra de cultura contemporània de barcelona	80
centre d'art santa monica	83
cineplex	132
claris	12
club 22	141
columbus	120
cometacinc	64
conectate	52
custo	109

d

danzatoria	141
discos edison's	91
do.bella	30
dom	51

e

e&a gispert	110
eixample, l'	36-55
els tres tombs	85
escribà	91

f

fc barcelona　　　　　　　138
formatgeria la seu　　　　　69
foro, el　　　　　　　　　104
forvm ferlandina　　　　　90
fountains　　　　　　　　136
fragile　　　　　　　　　　85
frederic marès　　　　　　60
freya　　　　　　　　　　33

g

gavina, la　　　　　　　　29
gente de pasta　　　　　　104
geomar　　　　　　　　　132
gimenez & zuazo　　　　　90
golondrinas　　　　　　　131
gotico, el　　　　　　　56-75
gràcia　　　　　　　　20-35
gran casino de barcelona　132
gran teatre del liceu　　　83

h

h10 racó del pi　　　　　　12
hispanoamericano　　　　　44
hivernacle　　　　　　　　104
hospital de la santa creu
i sant pau　　　　　　　　41
hostal de rita　　　　　　44
hostal mare nostrum　　　12
hotels　　　　　　　　11-17
hotel ac diplomatic　　　　11
hotel arts　　　　　　　　15
hotel banys orientals　　　11
hotel oriente　　　　　　　12
hotel sant agustí　　　　　15

i

iposa　　　　　　　　　　85

j

joan miró museum　　　　138
jordi olivé saperas　　　　30

k

kasparo　　　　　　　　　85
kennedy　　　　　　　　126
kwaleon　　　　　　　　110
kwatra　　　　　　　　　109

l

lailo　　　　　　　　　　91
limbo　　　　　　　　　　64
loft avignon　　　　　　　70
luz de gas　　　　　　　125

m

m40　　　　　　　　　　15
macba　　　　　　　　　80
madrid-barcelona　　　　　47
mandarina duck　　　　　48
manual alpargater, la　　　70
maremagnum　　　　　　129
mario　　　　　　　　　　29
marítim poliesportiu　　　131
masajes a 1.000　　　　　52
mercat de la boqueria　　　80
mercat de la concepció　　41
mercat de santa caterina　100
merendero de la mari　　125
metro　　　　　　　　　　18
mies & felj　　　　　　　91
miró jeans　　　　　　　73
modart　　　　　　　　　30

món de mones 33
montjuïc 136
muebles navarro 85
museu barbier-mueller
d'art precolombi 103
museu d'art contemporàni
de barcelona 80
museu d'història de catalunya 120
museu d'historià de la ciutat 60
museu de geologia 100
museu de la cera de barcelona 83
museu de la xocolata 100
museu de zoologia 100
museu gaudí 25
museu marítim 120
museu militar de montjuïc 138
museu nacional d'art
de catalunya 136
museu picasso 103
museu tèxtil i d'indumentarià 103

n
naftalina 30
ninas 33
nightlife 139-141
ninets 110

o
onno 109
original 85
oven 126, 141

p
palau dalmases 100
palau de justicia 99
palau de la música catalana 60
palau de la virreina 80

palau güell 83
paloma, la 139
papirum 69
parc de la ciutadella 113
parc güell 25
parc zoològic (zoo) 113
parkhotel 11
pas de la virreina 26
passeig de gràcia 41
pebre blau, el 108
pedrera, la 43
pintada 30
plà 64
pla dels àngels 85
plaça de la barceloneta 123
plaça de sant josep oriol 61
plaça del pi 61
placa portal de la pau 129
poble espanyol 139
port olímpico 141
pucca 107

r
ra 85
raval, el 76-95
reial club marítim de barcelona 125
replay 48
rey pez 73
rita blue 89
ruccula 125

s
sagrada familia 41
salero 107
salsitas 89, 141
sandwich & friends 107
santa església catedral

de barcelona	60
santa maria del mar	103
sesamo	85
sita murt	70
suite	33
sushi & news	89
system action	48

t

taira	104
tapa tapa	44
taverna del born, la	107
taverna estrella de gràcia	29
taxi	18
telefèric	131
tenorio	47
thai gardens	47
torres de ávila	139
tragaluz	47
transport	18-19
travelbar	67
tutto caffè	63

v

venus	64
vientos del sur	110
vila olímpica	116-133
vinya del senyor, la	108

w

| wok & bol | 47 |

z

zebra	69
zoo (parc zoològic)	113
zsu zsa	69

Category index

Food & drink

agua	125
bar amsterdam	44
bar kastola	26
bar terra	26
base nautica	126
bilbao-berria	63
buenas migas	63
cachitos	44
cafè de l'acadèmia	63
café del sol	29
cafe shilling	67
caffe di roma, il	46
cal pep	107
cantina machito	26
caracoles, los	67
carassa, la	108
cometacinc	64
els tres tombs	85
foro, el	104
fragile	85
gavina, la	29
gente de pasta	104
hispanoamericano	44
hivernacle	104
hostal de rita	44
iposa	85
kasparo	85
kennedy	126
limbo	64
luz de gas	125
madrid-barcelona	47
mario	29
merendero de la mari	125
muebles navarro 8	5
original	85
oven	126
pas de la virreina	26
pebre blau, el	108
plà	64
pla dels àngels	85
pucca	107
ra	85
reial club marítim de barcelona	125
rita blue	89
ruccula	125
salero	107
salsitas	89
sandwich & friends	107
sesamo	85
sushi & news	89
taira	104
tapa tapa	44
taverna del born, la	107
taverna estrella de gràcia	29
tenorio	47
thai gardens	47
tragaluz	47
travelbar	67
tutto caffè	63
venus	64
vinya del senyor, la	108
wok & bol	47

Hotels

claris	12
h10 racó del pi	12
hostal mare nostrum	12

hotel ac diplomatic	11
hotel arts	15
hotel banys orientals	11
hotel oriente	12
hotel sant agustí	15
m40	15
parkhotel	11

Neighborhoods

barceloneta & vila olímpica	116-133
borne, el	96-115
eixample, l'	36-55
gotico, el	56-75
gràcia	20-35
raval, el	76-95

Nice to do

antic hospital santa creu	93
aquarium, l'	131
biciclot	132
cineplex	132
conectate	52
geomar	132
golondrinas	131
gran casino de barcelona	132
masajes a 1.000	52
marítim poliesportiu	131
parc de la ciutadella	113
teleféric	131
zoo (parc zoològic)	113

Nightlife

poble espanyol	139
torres de ávila	139
paloma, la	139
café royale	139
danzatoria	141

port olímpico	141
salsitas	141
club 22	141
oven	141

Shopping

0,925	110
1748	109
armand basi	51
b.huno	91
bulevard rosa	51
caelumis	70
carhartt	109
casa del libre	48
casa miranda martì	70
casas	73
custo	109
discos edison's	91
do.bella	30
dom	51
e&a gispert	110
escribà	91
formatgeria la seu	69
forvm ferlandina	90
freya	33
gimenez & zuazo	90
jordi olivé saperas	30
kwaleon	110
kwatra	109
lailo	91
loft avignon	70
mandarina duck	48
manual alpargater, la	70
maremagnum	129
mies & felj	91
miró jeans	73
modart	30

món de mones	33	macba	80
naftalina	30	mercat de la boqueria	80
ninas	33	mercat de la concepció	41
ninets	110	mercat de santa caterina	100
onno	109	montjuïc	136
papirum	69	museu barbier-mueller	
pintada	30	d'art precolombi	103
placa portal de la pau	129	museu d'art contemporàni	
replay	48	de barcelona	80
rey pez	73	museu d'història de catalunya	120
sita murt	70	museu d'historià de la ciutat	60
suite	33	museu de geologia	100
system action	48	museu de la cera de barcelona	83
vientos del sur	110	museu de la xocolata	100
zebra	69	museu de zoologia	100
zsu zsa	69	museu marítim	120
		museu militar de montjuïc	138

Sights

antoni tàpies foundation	43	museu nacional d'art	
arc de triomf	99	de catalunya	136
camp nou	138	museu picasso	103
casa battló	43	museu tèxtil i d'indumentarià	103
casa milà	43	museu gaudí	25
casa vincens	25	palau dalmases	100
cccb	80	palau de justicia	99
centra de cultura		palau de la música catalana	60
contemporània de barcelona	80	palau de la virreina	80
centre d'art santa monica	83	palau güell	83
columbus	120	parc güell	25
fc barcelona	138	passeig de gràcia	41
fonteinen	136	plaça de la barceloneta	123
frederic marès	60	plaça de sant josep oriol	61
gran teatre del liceu	83	plaça del pi	61
hospital de la santa creu		sagrada familia	41
i sant pau	41	santa església catedral	
joan miró museum	138	de barcelona	60
la pedrera	43	santa maria del mar	103
		vila olímpica	123

Transport

bus turístic   18
cycling (biciclot)   132
metro   18
taxi   18

PARC GÜELL

This guide has been compiled with the utmost care. mo' media bv cannot
be held liable in the case of any inaccuracies within the text. Any remarks
or comments should be directed to the following address.

mo' media, attn. 100% barcelona,
p.o. box 7028, 4800 ga, breda, the netherlands, e-mail info@momedia.nl

author	nieke stein
translation	alex tobin @ burotexture
final editing	taunya renson-martin
photography	marieke hüsstege
graphic design	www.studio100procent.nl, naarden
cartography	eurocartografie, hendrik-ido-ambacht
project guidance	joyce enthoven & sasja lagendijk, mo' media
printing office	brepols, turnhout (b)

100% barcelona   isbn 90 5767 106 2 - nur 510, 512
© mo' media, breda, the netherlands, april 2003